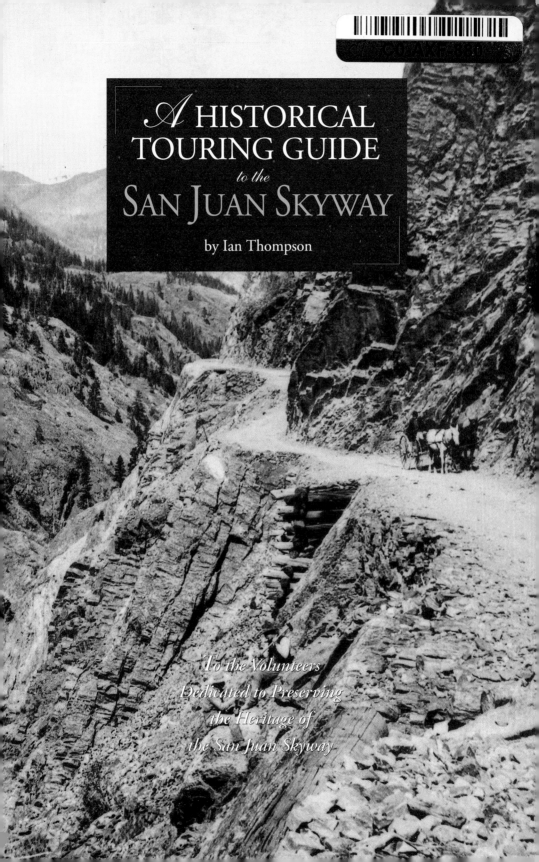

$\mathcal{A}$ HISTORICAL TOURING GUIDE
to the
SAN JUAN SKYWAY

by Ian Thompson

*To the Volunteers
Dedicated to Preserving
the Heritage of
the San Juan Skyway*

Why this Book was Produced

This Historical Touring Guide was created for Southwest Colorado residents and tourists who are interested in the history of the towns and places along the San Juan Skyway. The Guide is intended as an introduction to the region's past. Travelers are urged to visit the museums and visitors' centers in order to gain a deeper knowledge of each community along the Skyway.

Preserving Our Past

The cultural heritage along the San Juan Skyway is an irreplaceable treasure. Into it are woven centuries of human endeavor in a rugged and beautiful land, the San Juan Country. The first successful efforts to preserve this cultural heritage were made in the 1890's when local women, alarmed at the destruction by looters of the cliff dwellings at Mesa Verde, enlisted the help of women's clubs across Colorado and the nation and persuaded Congress to create Mesa Verde National Park.

Their campaign resulted, as well, in the passage of the Antiquities Act of 1906, protecting all archaeological sites on public lands. That preservationist tradition is continued today as historical societies all along the San Juan Skyway work to preserve the ancient, historical and modern heritage of the San Juan Country. Distribution of this book will hopefully further these preservation efforts.

Ken Francis, *Office of Community Services*
Fort Lewis College, Durango, Colorado

Title page photography: Otto Mears' toll road just south of Ouray on what is now the San Juan Skyway. (Courtesy, Colorado Historical Society, Neg. #F34,202)

Below: The Rio Grande Southern Railroad provided transportation for freight, ore and passengers to communities on the western side of the San Juan Mountains from 1890 to 1952. (Courtesy, Center for Southwest Studies, Fort Lewis College)

Copyright ©1994
Fort Lewis College
1000 Rim Drive
Durango, CO 81301-3999

INTRODUCTION:
THE SAN JUAN COUNTRY

The San Juan Skyway follows ancient Indian trails. It traces the routes taken by eighteenth century Spanish explorers when this was part of the Spanish empire. It follows rivers trapped by mountain men when this was part of Mexico. Sections of the Skyway were once pack trails blasted into cliffs by the pioneers of a westward expanding United States.

The Skyway winds over mountain passes, past Victorian mining towns, and through canyons so steep and rugged that they dashed the hopes of the nineteenth century railroad builders who wanted trains to run the entire route now followed by the San Juan Skyway. The road sweeps through vast cattle ranches shadowed by 14,000 foot peaks and skirts farms and orchards settled by gold seekers who rushed first to the fickle mountains then turned to a more stable existence homesteading the mesas and valleys below. The Skyway provides access to world class ski resorts and recreational areas, and it is Main Street to modern towns where old and new cultures blend to form a unique San Juan culture as the region moves into the twenty-first century.

The rich tapestry of Native history in the San Juan Country stretches back thousands of years. NonNative history began with the first recorded Spanish explorations just over two centuries ago. But in the San Juan Country even thousands of years are a tick of the clock.

SINCE THE BEGINNING...

In 236 miles (378 km), the San Juan Skyway traverses two billion years of visible geologic history. Oceans have come and gone leaving limestone and sandstone deposits thousands of feet deep. Mountain ranges have risen and been ground away, creating thick sedimentary layers atop the marine sediments. New mountains grew from the roots of the old and bent the overlaying sediments tens of thousands of feet upward into the sky. Glaciers erased even those mountains and the oceans returned laying down more sedimentary stone.

The final shallow sea slowly advanced and retreated across a landscape nearly erased of highlands. Dense fern forests, inhabited by dinosaurs, blanketed the coast lands. Slow rivers carried dying forests into coastal lagoons, forming the coal fields now surrounding the San Juan Mountains. The last dinosaurs died, and their liquefying remains seeped through the porous stone and gathered into pools of oil beneath the San Juan Basin to the south of the mountains. The land began rising for the final time, and volcanos fractured the ancient stone. Superheated liquid from deep in the earth boiled up into the cracks and cooled into veins of gold and silver ore far beneath the surface of the rising San

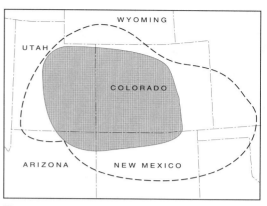

The traditional Ute territory covered an area larger than the State of Colorado.

The Brunot Agreement of 1873 took a strip of the San Juan Mountains from the Utes.

A treaty in 1868 created a Ute reservation less than half the size of the Utes' traditional territory.

The Ute Reservations today.

Juan Dome. At a later time, glaciers gouged chasms into the higher reaches of the dome, exposing the ore veins and their riches.

The climate warmed, the glaciers melted, and new forests claimed all but the highest elevations which even now remain above timberline. Thousands of years of winds blowing from the southwest, across the vast red lands of the Colorado Plateau, brought and deposited the red, fertile soils found on the mesas today. That process continues even now. Two billion years of geologic events are the primary shapers of human cultures in the San Juan Country even today.

The highest elevations, which get the most snow and rain and where frosts can occur every month of the year, are blanketed by treeless tundra. Below timberline the mountain slopes are forested by moisture-loving fir and aspen which give way to towering pines as the land descends. The mesas and lower valleys, which get the least moisture, are covered, in their natural state, by piñon, juniper, and sage. The peaks are wettest and coldest; the mesas are driest and warmest. The resulting ecological diversity contains ecosystems found from Alaska to northern Mexico.

he Ute Indians once occupied
most of what is now the State of
Colorado. (Courtesy, Colorado
Historical Society. Neg. # F7832)

The first people arriving in the San Juan Country, perhaps 10,000 years ago, cared nothing about coal fields, subterranean pools of oil, ores rich in precious metals, or the fertile mesa soils awaiting plows. They were attracted by the ecological diversity. They had no need to tame the wilderness. The wilderness fed, clothed, and housed them. They moved with the seasons. They travelled up the river valleys in spring, reached the cool peaks in summer, then followed the trails of game down toward the warmer mesas in autumn where they made their winter camps. They hunted and gathered as they moved through the rugged, nurturing land, pursuing their seasonal round. This way of life lasted here for thousands of years.

Farm plots were cleared and planted, and the first semi-permanent communities were settled along what is now the San Juan Skyway more than 2,000 years ago. The earliest farm hamlets known to archaeologists in the San Juan Country are in the vicinity of Durango. The first domestic plant grown was probably corn. Whether the earliest San Juan farmers were the hunting and gathering peoples who already lived here or were people migrating here from the south is not known. Farming spread quickly throughout the mesa elevations of the southern and western San Juan Country and new crops were added to corn. The population grew and communities slowly became more deeply rooted. Hunting and gathering continued to be important.

Today's Pueblo people are descended from the people who once lived in and near Mesa Verde. Courtesy, La Plata County Historical Society.

That early San Juan Puebloan culture here was dynamic and changed over time. Architecture became more substantial reflecting increasingly complex religious and social organization. Communities moved from place to place across the landscape. At times people lived in large villages and at other times they lived in smaller hamlets scattered across the mesas and along the streams. By the thirteenth century large masonry pueblos occupied the canyon rims and the cliff dwellings of Mesa Verde were under construction. By the end of the thirteenth century no Pueblo people remained in the San Juan Country. They had moved south and east to join other Puebloan people already living in what we now call New Mexico and Arizona. The Puebloan people are there today.

A view of Escalante ruin at the time it was being excavated. The twelfth century building, located on the grounds of the Anasazi Heritage Center at Stop One, is similar to at least seventy others found throughout the Four Corners region. (Courtesy, Bureau of Reclamation. Photo by Joan Fleetman)

SAN JUAN COUNTRY ECOSYSTEMS

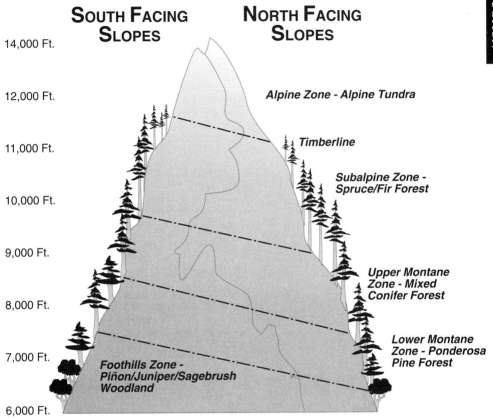

SOUTH FACING SLOPES

NORTH FACING SLOPES

14,000 Ft.

12,000 Ft. — *Alpine Zone - Alpine Tundra*

11,000 Ft. — *Timberline*

Subalpine Zone - Spruce/Fir Forest

10,000 Ft.

9,000 Ft.

Upper Montane Zone - Mixed Conifer Forest

8,000 Ft.

Lower Montane Zone - Ponderosa Pine Forest

7,000 Ft. — *Foothills Zone - Piñon/Juniper/Sagebrush Woodland*

6,000 Ft.

"This vast region of many thousand square miles is abrupt and broken, with an average elevation of 13,000 feet above the sea, with some of their peaks reaching the altitude of 14,500 feet. The scenery of such a section must necessarily verge nearer the sublime than any known in the world. Nature must have been in wild riot to have produced such a "wreck of matter" as is here found. If the ruins of ancient cities impress the beholder with wonder and amazement, what must be the emotions in viewing what one might imagine to be an exploded world, with its sharp broken fragments piled, in strange confusion, 14,000 feet high? The molten peaks are tinged with red and sulphurous hue, which tells of a period at which the chemical properties of the earth were made to gild each crest with rare, enduring colors."

"History of Colorado"
By W. B. Vickers in
HISTORY OF THE ARKANSAS VALLEY,
COLORADO, 1881

To Placerville

TELLURIDE

145

Stop
5

Telluride
Mountain
Village

Alta Lakes

Ophir

N

145

Trout Lake

Stop
4

**Lizard Head
Pass 10,222 ft.**

HOW TO USE THIS BOOK

This guide has been designed to accompany your tour through the San Juan Country and the San Juan Skyway. It is divided and indexed by towns and stretches of highway, so no matter where you happen to enter the Skyway loop you can easily identify your location and the corresponding pages in the guide.

Locater Map →

The locater map on the facing page shows the entire San Juan Skyway, the 12 major museum stops along the route, towns and significant landmarks like passes, divides, parks and interpretive overlooks. Note the page numbers beneath the stops and landmarks for easy referencing to match your location with the appropriate section of the guide.

← Left Hand Margin Maps

The left hand margin maps show sections of highway between towns, noting landmarks and other information for that section.

Caution and Safety

The San Juan Country is an exciting region to explore but safety and caution should always be a major concern. When driving, hiking or exploring pre-historic and historic sites remember, take nothing but pictures and leave nothing but footprints. It is illegal to remove artifacts of any sort. In addition, it is unsafe to explore unstabilized mills, mines and timber structures that are hazardous and decaying. Much of the property is private and should be afforded proper respect and restraint.

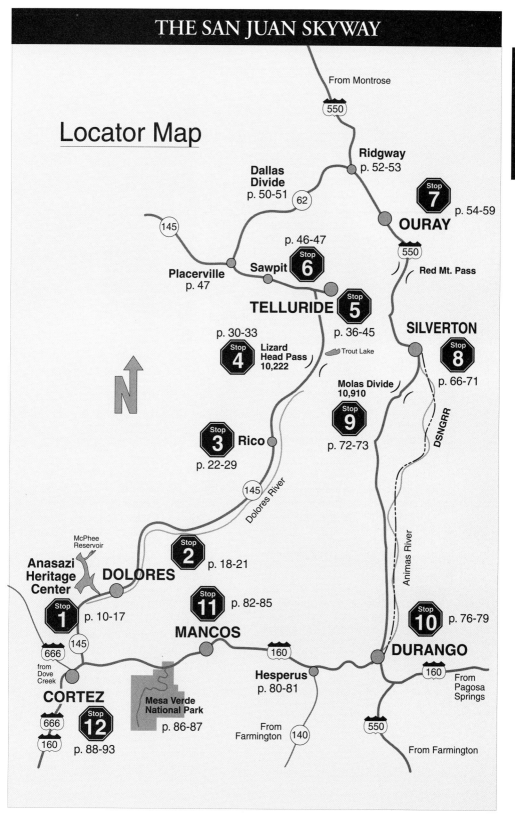

Locator Map

From Montrose

550

Ridgway
p. 52-53

Dallas
Divide
p. 50-51

62

145

p. 46-47

Stop 7
p. 54-59

OURAY

550

Placerville
p. 47

Sawpit

Stop 6

Red Mt. Pass

TELLURIDE **Stop 5**

p. 30-33

p. 36-45

SILVERTON

Stop 4

Lizard
Head Pass
10,222

Trout Lake

Stop 8
p. 66-71

Molas Divide
10,910

Stop 9
p. 72-73

DSNGRR

Stop 3 Rico

p. 22-29

145

Dolores River

McPhee
Reservoir

Stop 2 p. 18-21

Animas River

Anasazi
Heritage
Center

DOLORES

Stop 11 p. 82-85

Stop 1 p. 10-17

MANCOS

Stop 10 p. 76-79

DURANGO

666

145

160

160

from
Dove
Creek

Hesperus
p. 80-81

From
Pagosa
Springs

CORTEZ

Mesa Verde
National Park
p. 86-87

From
Farmington

140

550

From Farmington

666

Stop 12

160

p. 88-93

9

THE ANASAZI HERITAGE CENTER

STOP 1

THE ANASAZI HERITAGE CENTER

The Anasazi Heritage Center, located 2.4 miles (3.8 km) west of Dolores and 9.2 miles (14.7 km) north of Cortez on Highway 184, includes permanent exhibits depicting the archaeology of the area. Films, interactive computer programs, and temporary exhibits further interpret the ancient and modern cultures of the Four Corners region. A museum store features books on archaeology and Indian cultures. A .5 mile (.8 km) trail leads from the Heritage Center to Escalante Ruin. Museum hours are 9-5 daily. Closed Thanksgiving, Christmas, and New Year's days. Ruins hours are 8-5 daily, weather permitting. Admission is free. Handicapped accessible and captioned programs. The Anasazi Heritage Center is operated by the Bureau of Land Management.

Elevation 7,050 feet above sea level

Escalante Ruin sits atop a knoll on the grounds of the Anasazi Heritage Center. From the the knoll you will look down on McPhee Reservoir and the Dolores River Valley on the north and into the San Juan River.Basin on the south. Forty miles to the northeast is 14,240 foot Mount Wilson and to its right, Lizard Head. The peak and spire mark the headwaters of the Dolores River. At the foot of the knoll, the Dolores turns northward toward the Colorado River.

To the south you will see Mesa Verde and to its right, Sleeping Ute Mountain. Through a gap between Mesa Verde and Sleeping Ute Mountain, across the San Juan River, the Chuska Mountains are visible in Arizona and New Mexico. To the east are the 13,000 foot peaks of the La Plata Mountains and to the west the Great Sage Plain stretches to the horizon. The Abajo Mountains in Utah mark the northwestern edge of the Great Sage Plain.

From the top of Mount Wilson to the San Juan River the land drops more than 9,000 feet. You can see the peaks above timberline, the highest fir and aspen forests on the mountainsides, and then the pine forests (known as the Glades) sloping toward the Dolores River. You are standing in the pinyon, juniper, and sage zone of the Great Sage Plain. Through the gap in the south you can see the shrub and grasslands of the lowest elevations.

McPhee Reservoir was constructed in the 1970s and 1980s to store water for irrigating farmlands on the Great Sage Plain. During its construction scores of archaeologists conducted research in the area to be flooded. Artifacts and the records of that research are curated in the Anasazi Heritage Center.

"Upon an elevation on the river's south side, there was in ancient times a small settlement of the same type as those of the Indians of New Mexico, as the ruins which we purposely inspected show."

Fray Silvestre
Velez de Escalante
August 13, 1776

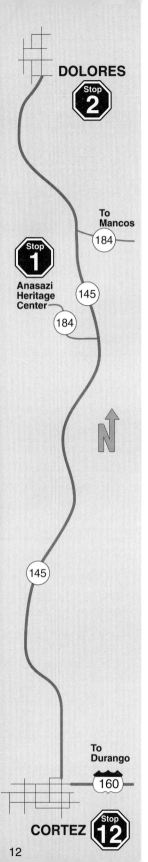

DOLORES

Stop 2

To Mancos
184

Stop 1

Anasazi Heritage Center

145

184

N

145

To Durango
160

CORTEZ Stop 12

12

THE ANASAZI HERITAGE CENTER *CONTINUED*

Puebloan farm settlements began appearing in the Dolores River Valley in the seventh century A.D. and, by the late ninth century, as many as 3,000 people may have occupied the valley in the vicinity of Escalante Ruin. Then they began to leave. By the middle of the tenth century, nearly two centuries before construction of the building now known as Escalante Ruin, the Dolores River Valley and much of the area surrounding the knoll was deserted. Perhaps people had moved south where the population of the Chuska Valley and Chaco Basin increased by more than threefold in the tenth century.

By the middle of the eleventh century, people were returning and building houses on the ridges east and west of the knoll but not on the valley bottom. Houses were built on the slopes of the knoll. One of them, Dominguez Ruin, at the entrance to the Heritage Center, is excavated and stabilized. Construction of the Escalante building, far larger than Dominguez Ruin or any of the other houses on the slopes below you, began around 1130 A.D. The location and architectural layout of the building resembles that of at least seventy similar buildings found in Chaco Canyon and

A Ute dancer. (Courtesy, Colorado Historical Society. Neg. # 25,707)

elsewhere throughout the vast San Juan River Basin. Many archaeologists believe that these great houses are part of a cultural phenomenon which began in Chaco Canyon and spread outward from there.

By late in the twelfth century the Escalante great house and the community on the slopes of the knoll were silent and deserted. However, the populations of the Great Sage Plain to the west and Mesa Verde to the south of you were growing. The final century of the Puebloan occupation of the San Juan Country had dawned. The towns of the Great Sage Plain and Mesa Verde were deserted by the end of the thirteenth century.

Visitors at Mesa Verde's Far View Ruins, circa 1920's. (Courtesy, San Juan National Forest)

West of Mesa Verde you can see Sleeping Ute Mountain rising to an elevation of nearly 10,000 feet. The mountain lies entirely within the boundaries of the modern Ute Mountain Ute Reservation. It is not known if the Utes were here at the same time as the San Juan Puebloans. If not, they weren't far away. Unlike the Puebloans, the early Utes were not farmers. They continued to pursue the annual seasonal round, between the peaks and the lower mesas and valleys, hunting game, gathering food plants, and making temporary camps along the way. At the time of the first official Spanish explorations in the late eighteenth century, the region surrounding the San Juan Skyway north of the San Juan River was firmly controlled by Ute bands.

The Archaeological Center of the U.S.

The San Juan Skyway provides access to a vast region that was home to the Pueblo Indians until the end of the thirteenth century. Ancient Puebloan public buildings and homes are now preserved on public and tribal lands throughout the Four Corners region of Arizona, Colorado, New Mexico, and Utah. They may be visited at Lowry Ruin west of Pleasant View, Colorado, the Ute Mountain Tribal Park, Mesa Verde National Park, Chimney Rock Archaeological Area, Aztec National Monument, Chaco Culture National Historical Park, Canyon de Chelly National Monument, Edge of the Cedars State Park, Navajo National Monument, Hovenweep National Monument, and at Salmon Ruin. All are within a one-day roundtrip from modern communities along the Skyway.

Excavation of Chacoan ruins atop mesa at Chimney Rock Archaelogical Area, late 1960's. (Courtesy, San Juan National Forest)

You can see the Chuska Mountains in Arizona and New Mexico. They lie entirely within the boundaries of the modern Navajo Nation, the largest and most populous Indian Nation in the United States today. The Navajos arrived in the country south of the San Juan River from the north, probably beginning in the fifteenth century.

In the late sixteenth century, Spain created the Province of New Mexico covering most of the American Southwest. The entire San Juan Country was within the borders of that province. A provincial capital was founded on the middle Rio Grande River in 1596 and moved a few miles south, to Santa Fe, in 1610. Spanish settlements were never established in the San Juan region controlled by the Utes but it is likely that the Spanish pioneers of New Mexico entered the region to trade with the Utes and to prospect for gold and silver. Many of the mountain ranges, peaks, rivers, and mesas still bear Spanish names. Utes obtained the horse from the Spanish and became formidable riders.

The first official Spanish exploration of what is now southwest Colorado occurred in 1765. Guided by Utes, the explorers followed ancient Indian trails, passing by the foot of the knoll where you are standing. A more ambitious exploration took place in 1776 when two priests, Dominguez and Escalante, sought to find a route from Santa Fe to newly established missions on the Pacific Coast, a route that avoided the Navajos to the south. The party camped near the knoll and Escalante climbed it and described the ruin that is here today.

Escalante Ruin at the Anasazi Heritage Center, Stop 1. The circular room in this structure is a kiva and was used for ceremonial as well as domestic purposes. This kiva is similar to those found in Chaco Canyon. (Courtesy, Anasazi Heritage Center)

In 1821, Mexico declared its independence from Spain and the San Juan Country was within Mexico's new borders. Fur trappers entered the region during that time. In 1848, after the Mexican-American war, Mexico ceded most of the Southwest, including the San Juan Country, to the United States. The Utes continued to control much of what is now Colorado and Utah. The first gold rush into

Ute Indians camped in Durango in the late 19th century. (Courtesy, The La Plata County Historical Society)

the Rockies began in 1858, 250 miles north of the San Juan Mountains. Colorado Territory was created, with Denver as its capital and the San Juan Country in its southwestern corner.

Dominquez Ruin at the Anasazi Heritage Center dates to the twelfth century and is typical of the small houses found throughout the region near Mesa Verde. (Courtesy, Anasazi Heritage Center)

15

THE ANASAZI HERITAGE CENTER *CONTINUED*

A treaty in 1868 created the Ute Reservation covering most of the western slope of the Rockies in Colorado, including the San Juan Mountains. The new reservation, which included a smaller Ute reservation in Utah, was much smaller than the original Ute domain. The United States government assured the Utes it would be solely theirs "as long as the grasses grow and the waters flow." Whites would not be allowed to trespass or settle on Ute lands, according to the terms of the agreement.

The lure of gold and silver in the San Juan Country proved stronger than the government's word. Within two years of the creation of the reservation, prospectors were crossing the Continental Divide into the high San Juans, penetrating deep into Ute land. The prospectors discovered the gold and silver bearing veins in the mountains. An illegal gold rush began. The Utes protested, and on two different occasions troops were ordered by President Ulysses Grant to remove the white trespassers. The orders were retracted both times when Colorado officials assured Washington that the

(Courtesy, Anasazi Heritage Center)

Utes would agree to give up the mineral-rich San Juans. Conferences with the Utes, however, ended with the Utes refusing to surrender any more territory.

Another attempt was made in 1873 to seek an agreement with the Utes which would open the San Juan Country to settlement. Though they had met many times before, the 1873 negotiations would assure a place in Colorado history for two men: Chief Ouray of the Utes and Otto Mears, the "Pathfinder of the San Juans". The chief government negotiator was Felix R. Brunot, President of the U.S. Board of Indian Commissioners. Chief Ouray was recognized by the government as chief spokesman for all the Ute bands. Not all the Utes agreed. The negotiations soon reached an impasse.

"Western Colorado, though, undoubtedly, the finest part of the State, is practically unproductive, owing to Indian occupation. The Indian Reservation is an immense body of fine mineral, pastoral, and agricultural land, larger than the State of Massachusetts twice over -nearly three times as large, in fact. It is nominally occupied by about 3,000 Ute Indians."

"History of Colorado"
by W.B. Vickers of the
ARKANSAS VALLEY COLORADO 1881

Chipeta, front row second from left, and her husband Chief Ouray, front row third from left, were Ute leaders at the time territorial leaders were calling for removal of the Utes from Colorado. Otto Mears, second row far right, was instrumental in negotiating the treaties and agreements which reduced the Ute Reservation to a thin strip of land south of the San Juan Skyway. This photograph was taken in Washington in 1874 at the signing of the Brunot Agreement. (Courtesy, Colorado Historical Society. Neg. # F1012)

Southwest Colorado now draws millions of visitors annually. They come for the history, cultures & adventure. (Courtesy, La Plata County Historical Society)

Otto Mears, a Russian immigrant and a friend of Ouray's, was consulted by Brunot. Mears agreed to join the negotiations and to speak with the Utes. Ouray was persuaded by Mears to agree to surrender four million acres in the San Juans. Ouray agreed to allow mining on "the

Steam engines near the Rio Grande Southern depot in Dolores. (Courtesy, Frank and Ruby Gonzales)

mountaintops" within the four million acres with the fertile valley bottoms being reserved for the Utes. Ouray persuaded his people of the necessity of the agreement. The Brunot Agreement was approved by Congress in early 1874 and the rush was on. The mountain tops soon rang with picks and hammers ... and the valley bottoms soon succumbed to the white man's plows. Ouray and Mears had just begun to make their mark on the history of Colorado.

For several years the newcomers' hold on the San Juan Country was tenuous at best. Supplies and mining gear were brought in by pack trains and ores were hauled out to distant smelters the same way. Thus, supplies and gear were costly and the price of such transport greatly diminished the miners' profits. Toll roads were constructed to provide access to teams and wagons but that did little to lower transportation costs. The solution would be railroads. The rugged Rocky Mountains posed a formidable challenge to railroad engineers.

The first tracks reached Durango in 1881 and their ultimate destination, Silverton, in 1882. The mining boom began in earnest. Abundant coal deposits fueled newly built smelters. The railroads expanded to more mountain mining camps, assuring their futures. One of those historic railroads passed within two miles of the knoll where you are standing now. The San Juan Skyway closely parallels the nineteenth century toll roads and railroads.

The trains did more than fuel the mining booms. The small low country farms that had been feeding the mining camps could now send their produce to larger markets. Vast ranches spread through the forests because cattle and sheep could be shipped to distant cities. Fir and pine trees could be hauled to sawmills and lumber shipped to build those cities.

The Weidman Sawmill, which was located just south of Durango, is now closed. However, its namesake, Sawmill Road, still remains. (Courtesy, San Juan National Forest)

Pack burros and a stagecoach on Cental Avenue, Dolores, in 1893. (Courtesy, Galloping Goose Historical Society. Photo by William Henry Jackson)

Thousands of tourists rode the rails every year to see the mountain splendor and the ancient ruins of the San Juan Country. The legacy of the railroads lingers. Today there is only one surviving community along the San Juan Skyway that has never been served by rail.

If you will look down the long, gradual slope to the south of the knoll you will see the town of Cortez several miles below in the Montezuma Valley. No railroad ever entered Cortez. It owes its birth and existence to an engineering marvel equal to that of the mountain railroads. In 1888 a tunnel was drilled beneath the dip in the ridge just east of the knoll and the waters of the Dolores River diverted by gravity flow into the Montezuma Valley.

Drilling for oil on the San Juan National Forest, 1937. (Courtesy, San Juan National Forest)

ANASAZI HERITAGE CENTER TO DOLORES

The sawmill in McPhee burned in 1948. (Courtesy, San Juan National Forest)

From the Anasazi Heritage Center the Skyway leads to the town of Dolores and follows the Dolores River into the high mountains where mining camps await you. The Galloping Goose Historical Society Museum is in the depot on the north side of the highway in the center of town. The Galloping Geese were a legendary fleet of gas-fueled automobiles converted for use on the tracks of the Denver and Rio Grande Southern Railroad which passed through Dolores. Between Dolores and Ridgway, the San Juan Skyway parallels the mountainous route of the Rio Grande Southern Railroad for 100 spectacular miles (160 km). You will visit the historic communities of Rico, Telluride, and Placerville—and much more along the way.

DOLORES

El Rio de Nuestra Senora de las Dolores, the words have a musical ring to them ... The River of Our Lady of Sorrows. The river may have been christened by the Spanish explorer Juan Rivera in 1765, or it may have been named that much earlier by Spaniards coming to trade with the Utes.

Dolores, like Ridgway and Durango, is a town that would never have existed had there never been railroads in the San Juan Country. Settlement of the Dolores River Valley in the vicinity of what was to become the town of Dolores began in the late 1870s. Most of the newcomers were homesteaders who cleared the land for crops and ran small herds of cattle in the nearby forests. In 1878 a cluster of homes, the community of Big Bend, began appearing in the valley bottom near the Escalante knoll where the Dolores River turns sharply northward. Soon there was a general store, a bank, a post office, and a school—all the necessary ingredients for permanence and a prosperous future. But that was not to be.

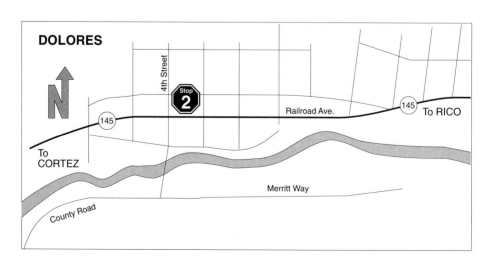

Fourth of July celebration in Dolores, 1893. (Courtesy, Colorado Historical Society. Neg. # F40489, The Rio Grande Collection.)

In 1889 plans were made by Otto Mears for a railroad running through and around the western flanks of the San Juan Mountains from Ridgway in the north to Durango in the south. The railroad would tap the riches accumulating in the booming mountain mining towns of Telluride and Rico and the smaller mining camps between the two towns. The 162 mile (270 km) railroad would, as well, link two segments of the Denver & Rio Grande Railroad coming into Durango from the east and into Ouray from the north. The new railroad would be known as the Rio Grande Southern.

STOP 2 - DOLORES

THE GALLOPING GOOSE MUSEUM

The museum operated by the Galloping Goose Historical Society of Dolores is located at 421 Railroad Avenue and is open May through October. It is housed in a replica of the town's original railroad depot. Museum exhibits feature the Rio Grande Southern Railroad and the history of Dolores and interpret the relationship between the two. A Galloping Goose, the gasoline powered rail car that carried passengers and freight on the Rio Grande Southern for decades, sits just outside the museum. Museum hours are 8 a.m. to 5 p.m. Monday through Saturday and 10 a.m. to 4 p.m. Sunday. Admission is free, but donations are accepted toward restoration of the Galloping Goose and other Historical Society projects. The Dolores Visitor Center is located in the same building. Elevation 6,957 feet above sea level.

The Galloping Goose on the Butterfly Trestle. The trestle was part of the Ophir Loop between Rico and Telluride. (Courtesy, Galloping Goose Historical Society)

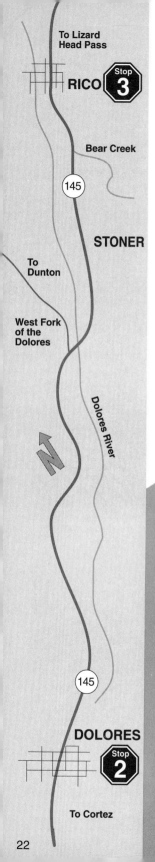

To Lizard
Head Pass

RICO · Stop 3

Bear Creek

145

STONER

To
Dunton

West Fork
of the
Dolores

Dolores River

N

145

DOLORES · Stop 2

To Cortez

Dolores River Valley

Mears was in a hurry. Every ton of ore hauled out of the mining camps by pack train was revenue lost to the new railroad. By 1891 more than 3,000 men were working on building the Rio Grande Southern. They worked from both ends toward the middle. They faced formidable engineering challenges. But the entrepreneurial Mears knew what he was doing; he'd been building toll roads and railroads in the San Juan Country for more than two decades when he took on the biggest project of them all, the Rio Grande Southern Railroad. The rails from Durango would enter the Dolores River Valley via Lost Canyon toward Rico. Big Bend was two miles down the Dolores River from the mouth of Lost Canyon.

In 1890 two Big Bend businessmen laid out the town site of Dolores at the mouth of Lost Canyon. The rest of the citizens of Big Bend soon followed. By the time the tracks reached Dolores on Thanksgiving Day, 1891, the community of Big Bend was no more.

Dolores was probably seen by the builders of the Rio Grande Southern as a watering stop along the way to Rico and its riches. And the first two booming years of the railroad's operation hauling thousands of cars of rich ore from the mountain mining camps would have strengthened that conviction. But Dolores would soon contribute more to keeping the Rio Grande Southern in operation for sixty years than any other town on the line.

If the railroad was born of the mining boom of the early 1890s, Dolores was born of the railroad. By the turn of the century, however, Dolores was at the center of a boom of its own. In 1902 two large timber companies built mills near Dolores. The nearest forests of towering Ponderosa pine soon vanished before the saws.

The sawmills closed. The history of the Dolores timber boom, however, was far from ended. The vast pine forests on the Glades remained untouched.

Mountainside forests were cleared to build the mining camps. (Courtesy, Colorado Historical Society. Neg. # F36418)

In 1924 the New Mexico Lumber Company began building Colorado's largest sawmill four miles down river from Dolores. A company owned railroad linked the new company town, named McPhee, to the Rio Grande Southern Railroad in Dolores. Work began immediately on a railroad which would snake through the Glades and bring logs to the new mill. Lumber production began in 1927. Despite the Great Depression, bankruptcies, ownership changes, mill fires, and World War II, millions of board feet of finished lumber rode the rails up to Dolores to be loaded onto Rio Grande Southern lumber trains headed for Durango and points beyond. The timber harvesting, milling, and company railroad operations employed hundreds of people.

Forests in the San Juan Country take many decades to grow back into harvestable timber. The timber harvests riding the rails into McPhee far outpaced the ability of the forests to renew themselves. Profits dwindled. On January 19, 1948, the big mill at McPhee burned.

Skiers at "Sky-Hi" Ski Hill, 1950. The ski area was closed in 1984 and rehabilitated to a natural state by the Forest Service. You can still see the old ski trails from the Skyway near Stoner. (Courtesy, San Juan National Forest).

23

DOLORES RIVER VALLEY

Traveling the West Dolores Road, 1926. Mt. Wilson in far background. Today, the West Dolores Road, which intersects the Skyway above Dolores, leads to several Forest Service campgrounds and the ghost town of Dunton. (Courtesy, San Juan National Forest)

The plants and railroad were scrapped and one of the Rio Grande Railroad's oldest customers was no more. The scrapping of the timber railroad was a harbinger of even larger railroad "salvage" operations soon to come. The company town site of McPhee is hidden today beneath the waters of McPhee Reservoir.

Timber was not the only freight loaded onto the Rio Grande Southern at Dolores. Another form of wealth grew there, grass. Tens of thousands of cattle and sheep ranged across hundreds of thousands of acres of high country in summer. In autumn they were driven to Dolores and loaded onto stock trains for the first leg of the journey to packing plants in distant cities. At the same time, orchards were spreading across the irrigated slopes of the Montezuma Valley to the south, and dryland fields of winter wheat and pinto beans were advancing across the deep red soils of the Great Sage Plain to the west.

In autumn the stockyards stretching along the rails in Dolores were crowded with cattle and sheep awaiting shipment. At the same time, huge apple sheds were filled to the roof beams with fragrant fruit, and elevators were filled with wheat and beans destined for distant markets. Dolores prospered.

Today the route of the Rio Grande Southern is buried beneath a wide stretch of Highway 145 passing through town one block

"The rush to the Dolores country has continued pretty much all summer, and a new town, named Rico, has been organized in the wilderness, with a newspaper and other adjuncts of civilized life."

"History of Colorado"
By W. B. Vickers in
HISTORY OF THE ARKANSAS VALLEY, COLORADO, 1881

McPhee, a company town associated with the largest sawmill in Colorado, was located three miles down river from Dolores. It is now under McPhee Reservoir. (Courtesy, Colorado Historical Society. Neg. #F23332)

Cowboy in the San Juan Mountains. (Courtesy, La Plata County Historical Society)

south of Central Avenue. Fire has taken its toll on the central business block in recent years, but two hotels and other historic structures are reminders of the days when ranchers, lumberjacks, and out-of-towners mingled in the Green Frog Saloon, and the banks were filled to the rafters with greenbacks.

Now, entering its second century, the economy of Dolores is still linked to agriculture, but sparkling McPhee Reservoir stretching ten miles down valley from the town limits has made the community into a lakeside recreation center as well. Small firms in Dolores manufacture quality products ranging from cider to backpacking equipment. The commitment of the community to preserving its past is seen in the new depot standing on the site of the old. It was built with volunteer labor and is a reminder that the Rio Grande Southern is gone but not forgotten. Dolores was born of the railroad, and Dolores sustained it for most of six decades.

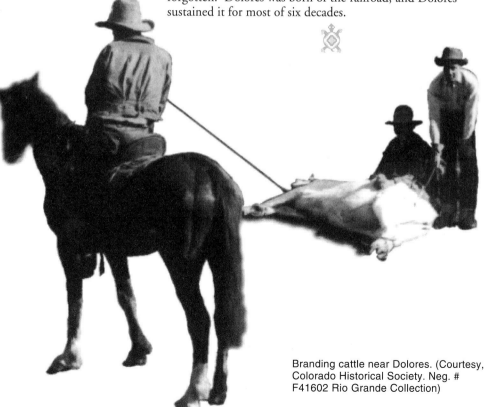

Branding cattle near Dolores. (Courtesy, Colorado Historical Society. Neg. # F41602 Rio Grande Collection)

The mines near Rico. (Courtesy, Colorado Historical Society. Neg. # F11032)

Rico

But countless trainloads of sheep, cattle, lumber, grain, and fruit were not what Otto Mears had in mind when his railroad reached Dolores from Durango and headed up the valley toward Rico. Mears' efforts would soon be richly rewarded.

The Dolores River Valley deepens as it climbs nearly 1,800 feet in elevation to Rico. Not far below Rico the peaks begin closing in and the valley becomes a canyon, widening briefly to allow room for a town before narrowing into a shadowy gorge above which the land levels into rolling meadows atop Lizard Head Pass. Today much of the valley floor between Dolores and Rico is occupied by historic cattle ranches. Until the ratification of the Brunot Agreement in 1874, it was a pristine wilderness deep in Ute territory.

In 1869, three prospectors trespassing on the Ute Reservation began removing small amounts of ore from the slopes above Rico. In 1872, more ore was illegally removed from the mountain sides overlooking the Dolores River. As it did everywhere, the discovery of gold and silver changed history. The wilderness would soon be transformed.

(Courtesy, Colorado Historical Society. Neg. # F31696)

Rico was indeed nearly inaccessible, far removed from the pack trails and wagon roads being pushed into the San Juan Mountains by Otto Mears and others. The town was founded in 1879 but its isolation continued to pose barriers to its founders' dreams.

Despite its remote location, within a month of its founding Rico boasted seven saloons, four assay offices, a sawmill, and a dairy farm to serve a population of 600 which had arrived virtually overnight.

THE RICO CENTER

The Rico Center is located on the west side of Highway 145 and is open from approximately May 1 to October 1.   The Center is staffed by volunteers who are knowledgable about Rico and the surrounding area. Ore samples from local mines, old photographs, and railroad spikes are on display in the Center. It includes a gift shop offering local crafts and a thrift shop. A walking tour map of historic Rico is available as are Forest Service maps and a brochure describing Rico, past and present. Hours are 10 a.m. to 4 p.m. daily and noon to 4 p.m. Sundays. Admission is free and so is the coffee.

Elevation 8,737 feet above sea level.

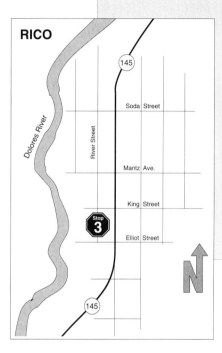

Rico railyards after the flood of October, 1911. (Courtesy, Colorado Historical Society. Neg. # F36413)

Hose team racers in the Rico fire department about 1886. (Courtesy, Colorado Historical Society. Neg. # F24569)

RICO *CONTINUED*

They prospected while they waited. The slopes surrounding Rico were soon covered with a patchwork of claims and small mining operations. In 1881 work began on a shaft at the Enterprise Mine high above the town to the south. The mine's owner, David Swickheimer, hoped the shaft would intercept the rich Swansea vein that surfaced not far away. In 1883 he ran out of money before reaching the vein. He tried again in 1887 but quickly ran out of money. His wife spent a dollar on a lottery ticket and won $4,000. She invested it in her husband's hopes. He went back to work on the Enterprise shaft and in October, 1887, struck the rich Swansea vein 262 feet below the top of the shaft. The Enterprise would take its place in Colorado history as one of the richer mines in the state.

A forest ranger heads out into the high country of the Montezuma National Forest, 1926. (Courtesy, San Juan National Forest)

"Rico is situated in the center of a volcanic outburst which has parted the sandstones and limestones once spread thousands of feet thick over the area, and whose edges now stand as bold bluffs all around this break, which is nearly four miles in breadth and about eight in length. The town itself is made of a scattered, garden less collection of log cabins and some frame buildings, with a log suburb called Tenderfoot Town ... everybody is waiting until the railroad gets a little nearer"

THE CREST OF THE CONTINENT
Ernest Ingersoll, 1885

Rico with the mines above it. (Courtesy, Colorado Historical Society. Neg. # 2843 photograph by William Henry Jackson)

"Rico means "rich," and undoubtedly the town is rightly named, for the camp is far in advance of what Leadville was at the same age. Of course, nobody knows what an undeveloped mining town will amount to one, two, or three years hence; but at present the Dolores country is looking up, its promise is all that could be desired. It is still comparatively inaccessible except by the rough mountain roads of the southwest; but there will eventually be a railroad in that direction....

"The History of Colorado"
By W. B. Vickers in
HISTORY OF THE ARKANSAS VALLEY, COLORADO, 1881

The Rio Grande Southern Railroad would soon scale a dizzying, vertical landscape to reach the rich new mines of Rico. The first train rolled into Telluride on Thanksgiving Day, 1890, on a branch line from the Rio Grande Southern's main route. Ten months later the first train rolled into Rico on September 30, 1891.

The cost of hauling ore out of Rico, Telluride, and surrounding mines dropped as much as ninety percent. Rio Grande Southern trains ran around the clock hauling silver bearing ore down out of the mountains and supplies up into the mountains. Two passenger trains a day made round trips between Rico and Ridgway and Rico and Durango. Rico boomed.

Rico in 1881. (Courtesy, Colorado Historical Society. Neg. # F21117)

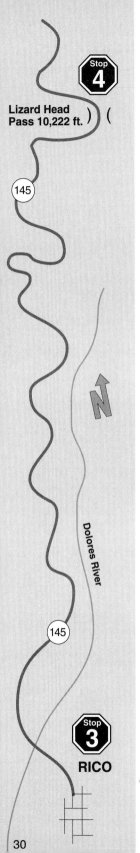

Stop
4

Lizard Head Pass 10,222 ft.

145

145

Stop
3

RICO

Dolores River

Rico - Lizard Head Pass

The mines, mills, and railroad operated twenty four hours a day. Rico never slept. Mining and railroad fortunes grew with each passing hour. Surely there were no limits to Rico's growth and prosperity, to the economic boom touched off by the coming of the railroad.

Fifty years later Rico was home to the woman, State Representative Elizabeth Pellet, who would lead the battle to keep the by then beleaguered Rio Grande Southern Railroad alive.

Before leaving Rico you should take a stroll up and down the streets that climb the hills from the Dolores River toward the mines. Below the San Juan Skyway, Highway 145 through Rico, you will find traces of the rail yards along the Dolores River, including a wooden water tank similar to dozens of such tanks once present along the Rio Grande Southern. Above the Skyway are the historic Dolores County courthouse, churches, and Victorian cottages that once looked down on, in every sense of the phrase, the rows of saloons and dance halls where the music never stopped. Stand quietly and listen carefully, the sound of barroom pianos and brass bands echoes from the peaks, harmonizing with dying echoes of whistling steam engines.

The first automobiles along the San Juan Skyway were their own snowplows. Today highway crews clear snow around the clock during winter snows. (Courtesy, Center for Southwest Studies).

STOP 4 - LIZARD HEAD PASS

SUMMIT OF LIZARD HEAD PASS

Immediately west of the summit of Lizard Head Pass is a point of interest and rest stop built and maintained by the United States Forest Service. The stop includes a photographic exhibit describing the historic importance of Lizard Head Pass and the Rio Grande Southern Railroad.

Elevation 10,250 feet above sea level.

Logging operation on Lizard Head Pass, 1913. (Courtesy, San Juan National Forest)

Look up the mountainside to the east and southeast and you will see the portal of the Enterprise Mine and other mines which fueled the silver boom that built Rico. More remnants of Rico's boomtown days may be seen across the river at the north end of town as you begin your ascent up the Dolores River toward the summit of Lizard Head Pass. Rico today is home to a handful of oldtimers who wouldn't live anywhere else and to a number of newcomers attracted by the mountain beauty. The mines are silent.

On leaving Rico, the Skyway climbs steeply before emerging into a broad, sloping meadow. The Wilson Mountains and Lizard Head, a freestanding spire of stone 13,113 feet above sea level, come into view to the west. Nine and a half miles (15.2 km) northeast of Rico, the Skyway reaches the summit of Lizard Head Pass. At 10,250 feet above sea level, Lizard Head Pass is the highest point on the route of the Rio Grande Southern.

Rio Grande Southern train at the summit of Lizard Head Pass. (Courtesy, Colorado Historical Society. Neg. # 2840 photograph by William Henry Jackson.)

LIZARD HEAD PASS TO TROUT LAKE

Highways can go where railroads cannot. They can negotiate much steeper grades and much sharper turns. Because it is possible for the modern traveller to safely drive up or down many of the steep grades on Lizard Head Pass at 55 miles per hour, it is difficult to imagine the challenges facing railroad builders who had to find much gentler routes on which to lay track. Keep this challenge in mind as you descend to the northeast from the summit of Lizard Head Pass. The Skyway follows a nearly straight line for less than two miles (3.2 km) to Trout Lake immediately east of the highway and continues past the lake in a straight line on down the valley. The elevational difference between the summit and the lake is a mere 450 feet.

A steam driven rotary plow clears the Rio Grande Southern tracks near Ophir. (Courtesy, La Plata County Historical Society.)

The railroad route did not go by the lake, it went around it, gradually gaining elevation as it went. The trains travelled more than 4 miles (6.4 km) to gain the same elevation as the highway does in less than two miles. By turning on to the gravel road along the northeast shore of Trout Lake you can follow the old railroad bed past an old water tower toward a surviving railroad trestle beyond the lake.

Sheep ranchers depended on the Rio Grande Southern to transport their stock out of the mountains each autumn. (Courtesy, San Juan National Forest.)

Finding a route from Trout Lake to the summit of Lizard Head Pass was relatively easy for the builders of the Rio Grande Southern. The ultimate challenge was met at nearby Ophir through construction of the Ophir Loop, the unequalled engineering triumph of the builders of the Rio Grande Southern.

One-and-a-half miles (2.4 km) northeast of Trout Lake, the Skyway passes old mining structures above and along the road. These are the remains of the mining camp of Matterhorn. Matterhorn's mining future was quickly eclipsed by the flourishing, nearby communities of Rico and Ophir. In the 1940s, Matterhorn gained a brief new lease on life as the shipping point for spruce timber to the lumber mills at McPhee near Dolores.

Matterhorn sits on the edge of the abyss. From here the Lake Fork of the San Miguel River plunges precipitously into a 1,000 foot deep canyon that continues to deepen as the river cascades on toward Vance Junction. Ophir sits on the edge of a tributary stream

Trout Lake, near the summit of Lizard Head Pass, was part of one of the first hydroelectric power systems in the world. (Courtesy, Center for Southwest Studies, Fort Lewis College)

entering the Lake Fork near Ames in the canyon bottom. The supreme challenge facing the builders of the Rio Grande Southern was how to get the railroad out of the canyon and on up the mountainside past Ophir to Matterhorn.

The Butterfly Trestle on the Ophir Loop. (Courtesy, Colorado State Historical Society, Neg. #F36,412)

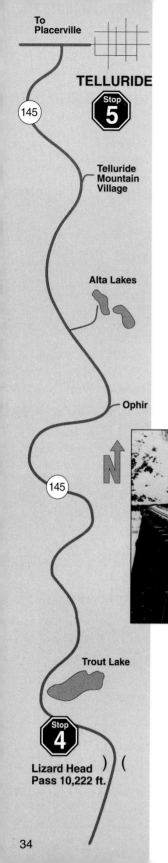

145

Telluride
Mountain
Village

Alta Lakes

Ophir

145

N

Trout Lake

Stop
4

Lizard Head
Pass 10,222 ft.

TROUT LAKE TO OPHIR

Not far above Vance Junction the railroad began inching up the western wall of the canyon, opposite Ophir and the route of the Skyway today. In the summer of 1891, when the tracks neared Ophir, the challenge was to get them across the deep canyon. A high, curving, wooden bridge, or trestle, nearly 500 feet long was built to span the canyon. The rails then crept up the wall of the tributary canyon and across yet another high trestle bridging the tributary. The rails looped around at Ophir and began climbing the wall of the tributary canyon directly above the rails approaching Ophir. The rails re-entered the Lake Fork canyon and climbed the east wall of that canyon to Matterhorn.

Many segments of the Ophir Loop and the "highline" on to Matterhorn are on narrow rock shelves blasted out of the sheer cliffs themselves. In places the trains rocked slowly along these niches above sheer thousand foot drops to the canyon floor below. Between Matterhorn and Ophir the modern San Juan Skyway roughly parallels the Rio Grande Southern route. The highway occupies its own shelf in the canyon wall a few yards above the old railroad right-of-way.

The trestles and tracks are gone now, but at Ophir you may wish to stop and contemplate the awesome engineering challenges overcome here. The Ophir Loop was a monument to the mining pioneers of the silvery San Juan who stood always ready to risk their necks and fortunes to remove more wealth from these mountains.

At Ophir a gravelled road plunges down the tributary canyon into the canyon of the Lake Fork of the San Miguel River. The road leads past Ames, another landmark in the engineering history of the San Juan Country, and, in this case, the engineering history of the world.

Ames was the location of the world's first alternating current power plant to generate electricity for industrial use, providing power to the mill at the Gold King Mine 2.6 miles up the mountainside above Ophir.

The Galloping Goose on the Ophir Loop, 1933. (Courtesy, Colorado Historical Society. Neg. #F23348)

Ruins of the old Chattenooga mining camp still stand today alongside the Skyway as it winds north up Red Mountain Pass. (Courtesy, San Juan National Forest.)

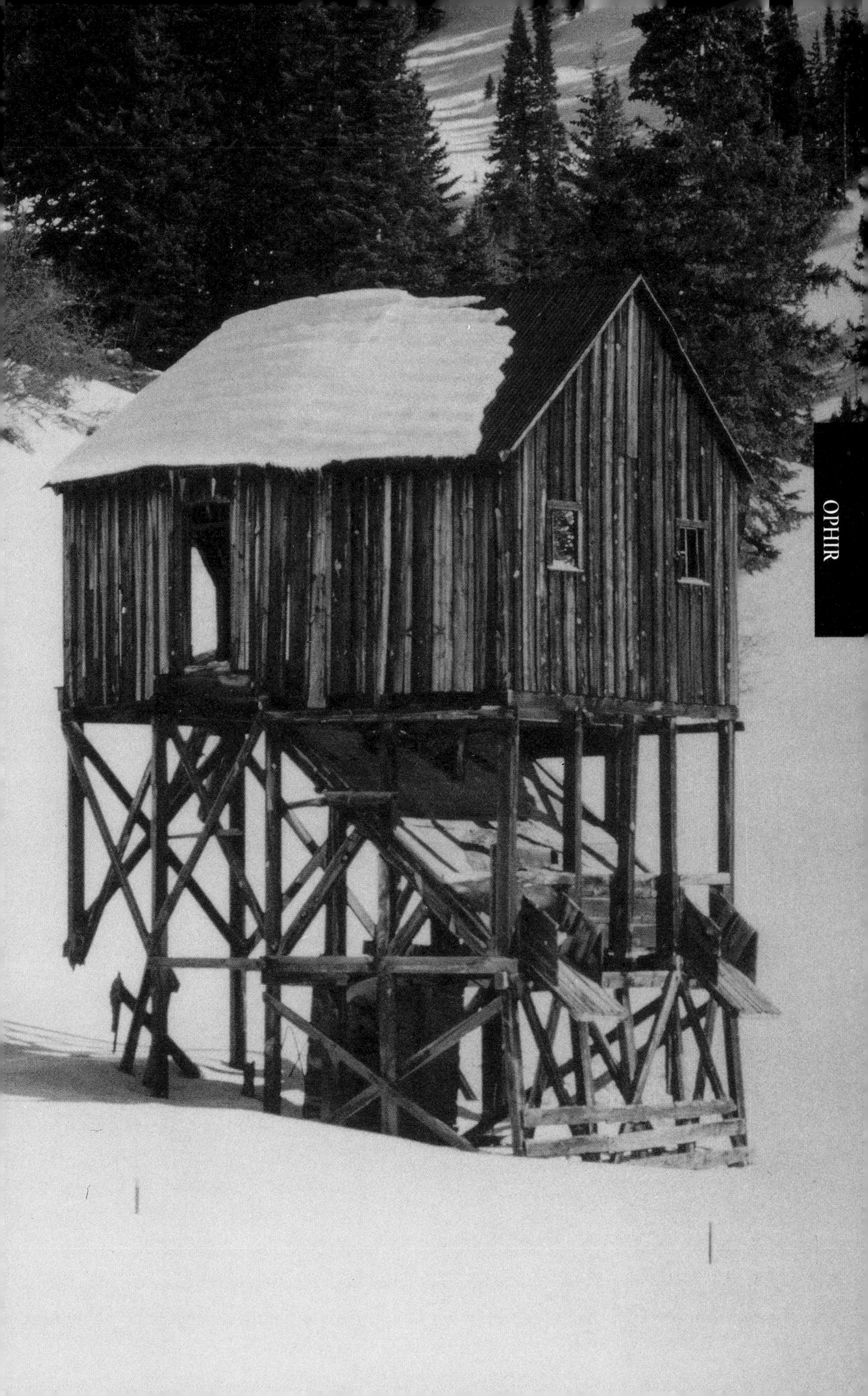

OPHIR TO TELLURIDE

L.L. Nunn, manager of the Gold King Mine and builder of the Ames Power Plant, had operated the mill with a coal-fueled steam engine. He hauled the coal by mule train up the mountain to the mill at a cost of $2,500 per month. Copper wire replaced the mules and his hydroelectric plant at Ames supplied power at a cost of $500 per month. Nunn went on to become a world leader in the new electrical power industry and eventually built the enormous hydroelectric plant at Niagra Falls, but not before he converted many San Juan Country mines and towns to the new form of energy. The Ames Power Plant continues in operation today.

Pack train in old Ophir at the turn of the century. (Courtesy, Center for Southwest Studies, Fort Lewis College)

From Ames, return to the San Juan Skyway at Ophir, and continue north toward Telluride. There is a wide pulloff on the west shoulder of the highway 1.75 (2-8 km) miles north of Ophir. This is a good place to stop and look west across the canyon of the Lake Fork and see the roadbed of the Rio Grande Southern clinging to the opposite wall of the gorge. Looking to the south, you can see where a huge trestle, now gone, once carried the tracks across the canyon toward Ophir.

Continuing toward Telluride you will descend past the entrance to Telluride Mountain Village which is part of the modern Telluride Ski Resort. Across the valley, just ahead, the Telluride airport can be seen suspended high above the San Miguel River. The Skyway descends steeply into the valley and levels briefly before crossing the San Miguel. The intersection is located at Society Turn, and Telluride can be seen nearly four miles up the valley. Society Turn took its name from the practice by Telluride's leading citizens of driving their carriages down valley on Sunday afternoons as far as Society Turn before turning back homeward. From Society Turn drive into Telluride.

The Ames Power Plant (Courtesy, Center for Southwest Studies, Fort Lewis College)

A view of Telluride from Society Turn (Courtesy, La Plata County Historical Society)

Settlement at the head of the San Miguel River began in earnest in 1875. By 1879 a placer operation at Keystone at the west end of the park was washing the gold dust from the gravel deposits above the river bed. There may have been gold dust in the gravel but it was the veins of silver bearing ore high on the steep mountain slopes above the upper San Miguel River Valley which

A forest ranger enjoys the scenery with visitors to the Montezuma National Forest, 1926. (Courtesy, San Juan National Forest.)

shaped the early history of Telluride. The town, temporarily known as Columbia, was founded in 1878 and assigned a post office in 1880. The name Telluride is taken from an ore combining the element tellurium with a high gold content and some silver. Ironically, tellurium the ore does not occur in the immediate vicinity of Telluride the town.

STOP 5 - TELLURIDE

THE TELLURIDE MUSEUM

The Telluride Historical Museum sits at the top of Fir Street and currently houses a collection of photographs and artifacts from Telluride's mining past. However, Telluride's history is not limited to mining. Utes used the valley for hunting and now Telluride is a booming resort community. Today, the Museum is expanding its exhibits to incorporate the voices of all the people for whom Telluride has been and is meaningful. The Telluride Visitor's Guide includes a walking tour past historic structures. The Museum is open weekdays from 10 a.m. to 5 p.m. Admission is $4. Proceeds are used to expand the Museum's exhibits and programs.

Elevation 8,756 feet.

TELLURIDE

To Telluride Airport — 145 — Galena Ave. — Columbia Ave. — Colorado Ave. — Pacific Ave. — Fir St. — Pine Street — San Miguel River — Stop 5 — Tomboy Road — FS 869 — 145 — Bear Creek Road FS 635 — N

TELLURIDE

Despite the wealth hidden beneath the surface of its mountains, Telluride and the San Miguel region suffered the usual slow start resulting from isolation. In 1881 Otto Mears provided some relief when his toll road from the town of Dallas in the Uncompahgre River Valley reached Telluride before continuing on to Ophir and its intended destination, Rico. With the completion of each of his toll roads, wagons loaded with ore could go where only burros and mules packing ore had gone before. But hauling unprocessed ore by wagon was still expensive and continued to eat into mine owners' profits.

Placer mining washed gold from gravels along the San Miguel River between Telluride and Placerville in the 1870's. (Courtesy, Denver Public Library, Western History Department)

"In this county lies the San Miguel gold district, occupying the mountains and stream of a tract of country forty miles broad by some seventy long ... This region began to be developed in 1875, at which time the attention of miners was drawn thereto by successful discoveries of rich placer diggings, creating a lively excitement. All along the San Miguel River and its forks and tributaries are extensive gravel deposits, rich in gold. These are being worked, some by companies on a large scale."*

"History of Colorado"
By W.B. Vickers in
HISTORY OF THE ARKANSAS VALLEY, COLORADO, 1881

Often, right on the heels of Mears, came another San Juan Country transportation legend, the freighter Dave Wood. Wood's wagon trains hauled supplies into the mining camps and mines, including those in the San Miguel River Valley, and they hauled ore out. The day to day existence of many mining camps and mines depended directly upon Woods' abilities. When he could figure out a way to shortcut one of Mears' toll roads, Woods built his own wagon roads. Woods headquartered in the town of Dallas and the day would come when Mears would exact costly, if unintentional, revenge on the upstart Woods.

Isolation was not the only challenge to the permanence of Telluride and other San Juan Country silver mining towns. The price of silver was notoriously fluid. The precious metal would be in fashion in good times, then slip from fashion in economic hard times. Gold, on the other hand, was purchased by the U.S. government—the price was pegged at $20 per ounce on the world market—and used to back its currency. Silver investors saw this as a form of government subsidy stabilizing the price of gold and demanded equal treatment.

In 1890, with passage of the Sherman Silver Purchasing Act, the silver investors got what they wanted. The Act provided for the purchase of all silver bullion produced in the nation, estimated at 4,500,000 ounces per month, at the going price. In 1890, the going price was

Freighters in Telluride. (Courtesy, Colorado Historical Society. Neg. # 5852)

Rio Grande Southern Railroad excursion train near Hesperus, circa 1900. (Courtesy, Center for Southwest Studies, Fort Lewis College)

Silver pass issued in 1889 by Otto Mears for use on his Silverton Railroad. (Courtesy, Colorado Historical Society. Neg. # F1214)

A miner in winter. (Courtesy, La Plata County Historical Museum)

$1.06 per ounce. Silver was king in the San Juan mining camps. With passage of the Act, investors in San Juan silver mines became wealthy overnight. Only one barrier remained to fulfilling the dreams of the town builders of the high San Miguel Valley, the lack of cheap transportation.

The first Rio Grande Southern train rolled into Telluride in 1890. Telluride, in the valley below the mines, boomed. Those mines—the Tomboy, the Smuggler-Union, the Sheridan, among many—became legendary and their managers and absentee owners became fabulously rich and powerful. Their local legacy is the beautiful Victorian architecture that survives in Telluride to this day.

TELLURIDE *CONTINUED*

The Rio Grande Southern Railroad—not his first or only railroad—made Otto Mears rich. In 1892 he had silver filigree railroad passes designed by a Santa Fe jeweler and gave away more than 500 of them to favored customers and friends. He gave away three solid gold passes on his railroads that same year. Mears was an investor in mines and in town sites, as well as in toll roads and railroads. For Mears, 1892 was a very good year.

The written history of many mining towns is dominated by those who struck it rich or subsequently got rich. They lived in

Wagon Train, Telluride, Colorado about 1880. (Courtesy, Center for Southwest Studies, Fort Lewis College)

Miners at the Smuggler Mine, Telluride. (Courtesy, Colorado Historical Society. Neg. # F6825 photograph by Barnhouse and Moore, Grand Junction, Colorado)

mansions, traveled in private railroad cars, and wielded great power. They socialized with one another and with no one else. But the owners and absentee investors were not in the chill, wet, dark shafts and tunnels blasting the ore from the surrounding rock.

The miners worked deep below the surface in mines whose portals were as high as 12,000 feet above sea level. They worked ten or twelve hour shifts in mines and mills that ran around the clock. They lived in boarding houses precariously attached to plunging mountainsides. In the winter the snow buried the landscape and the trails down to the towns. The miners lived always on the brink of death ... premature dynamite blasts, fatal gas, underground fires, avalanches, falls, cave-ins, pneumonia. Many died young, leaving widows and orphans in tents and shanties with nothing. The miners earned $3.50 a day ... or less. They had no mansions, private rail cars, nor power. They are often absent from the history of the mining camps.

The Smuggler-Union mill at Pandora, near Telluride. (Courtesy, Colorado Historical Society, Neg. # F6726)

But in the history of Telluride there is a chapter about the working man written by the working men. In 1896, the Western Federation of Miners chartered a union in Telluride. In 1899, most of the mines granted workers $3 a day for an eight hour day less $1 per day boarding costs. Millworkers did not benefit from this "windfall."

One mine, the Smuggler-Union, held out against the better pay and working hours. On May 4, 1901, union members at the Smuggler-Union Mine went on strike. They wanted $3 a day for an eight hour day. The management of the Smuggler-Urdon ignored the strikers and hired strikebreakers for ... $3 a day for an eight hour day. That should have been the end of unions in Telluride. It wasn't. The impasse triggered years of management-labor conflict.

Presidential candidate, William Jennings Bryan campaigning in Telluride. Bryan opposed repeal of the silver standard. (Courtesy, Center for Southwest Studies, Fort Lewis College)

TELLURIDE *CONTINUED*

A shoot out between strikers and strikebreakers on July 3, 1901, left one striker and two strikebreakers dead and three wounded including the mine superintendent. After a truce disarmed the strikebreakers, they were beaten and run out of the valley by union members. In 1902, the manager of the Smuggler-Union was assassinated in his living room. In 1903, millworkers walked off the job and sympathetic mine workers soon followed. Six carloads of state militia men were sent by Colorado's governor into Telluride. Strikers were loaded into railcars and dumped at Ridgway with warnings not to return. Many did. The strike continued until November 29, 1904, when the Western Federation of Miners conceded defeat. The mine owners and sympathetic merchants, backed by armed militia men, had outlasted the by then poverty stricken mining families. Even so, the workers of Telluride had written themselves into history.

"BANK" sign marks San Miguel Valley Bank that was robbed by Butch Cassidy and the Wild Bunch on June 24, 1889. (Courtesy, Telluride Historical Museum)

Today the mines overlooking Telluride are silent. The decline began soon after the strike was broken and lingered for decades. Today, the aerial trams leading up the mountains do not carry ore and miners. They carry skiers up one of the world's best ski mountains. The parks and halls that once rang with the oratory of Populists, Socialists, and union leaders today resound to bluegrass, jazz, film, and mountain festivals. Snow, the bane of miners, is cheered in modern Telluride and ideas, not silver, are the new source of wealth.

Before leaving Telluride, you should drive two miles (3.2 km) east to Pandora at the upper end of the valley near the bottom of Bridal Veil Falls. Pandora was a milling town with large mills processing ores from the Tomboy, Smuggler-

Workers in the Ames Power Plant. (Courtesy, Center for Southwest Studies, Fort Lewis College)

Union, and Sheridan mines among others. The mines were in the high peaks and basins north of Pandora. Ore was delivered from the mines to the mills by wagons, aerial trams, and mining trams. Processed ores were loaded onto Rio Grande Southern Railroad cars here for transport to distant smelters. Look up at the canyon walls to the north and east. You will see the network of roads and trails that led from the mines to Pandora and Telluride. The structure at the top of Bridal Veil Falls is a power plant that once provided electricity to the mills and Telluride.

Returning to Society Turn, travel west past the intersection toward Placerville.

(Courtesy, Center for Southwest Studies, Fort Lewis College)

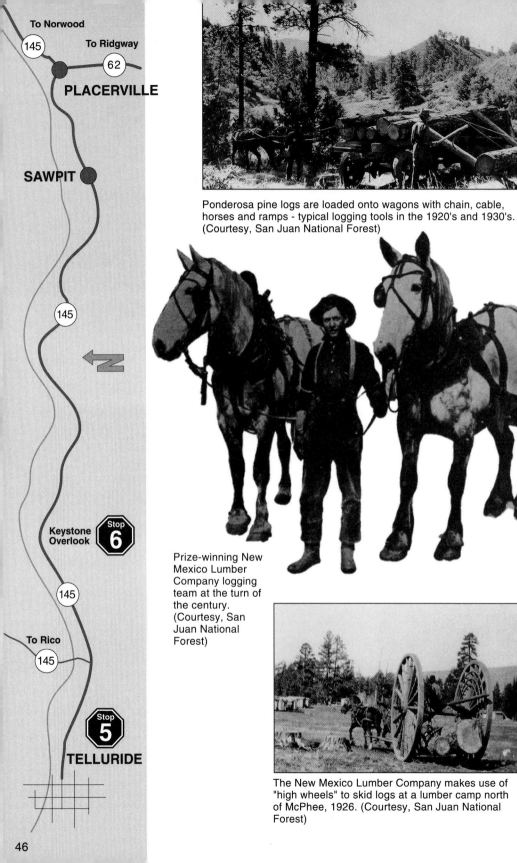

To Norwood

145

To Ridgway

62

PLACERVILLE

SAWPIT

145

N

Keystone
Overlook

Stop
6

145

To Rico

145

Stop
5

TELLURIDE

Ponderosa pine logs are loaded onto wagons with chain, cable, horses and ramps - typical logging tools in the 1920's and 1930's. (Courtesy, San Juan National Forest)

Prize-winning New Mexico Lumber Company logging team at the turn of the century. (Courtesy, San Juan National Forest)

The New Mexico Lumber Company makes use of "high wheels" to skid logs at a lumber camp north of McPhee, 1926. (Courtesy, San Juan National Forest)

STOP 6 - KEYSTONE OVERLOOK

KEYSTONE OVERLOOK
& TELLURIDE
INTRODUCTION SITE

Half a mile past the intersection on the south side of the Skyway is the Keystone Overlook and Telluride Introduction Site maintained by the United States Forest Service. The Overlook is at the top of Keystone Hill, named for a hydraulic placer mining operation that began in 1879 in the canyon downstream from the Overlook. Elevation 8,650 feet above sea level.

A Rio Grande Southern Railroad train begins the steep 7% grade to climb into Telluride via the Ilium Loop. (Courtesy, Colorado Historical Society)

TELLURIDE to PLACERVILLE

Traveling west from the Keystone Overlook, the Skyway descends quickly to the San Miguel River and its red-walled canyon. Eight miles (12.8 km) west of the Overlook is the hamlet of Sawpit, named for the creek flowing through it into the San Miguel. Sawpit sprang into existence in 1895 with the discovery of the Champion Belle vein. Hundreds of prospectors rushed into the area and the town site was laid out.

Four miles (6.4 km) west of Sawpit the Skyway enters the community of Placerville, elevation 7,321 feet. The town site was laid out in 1877 and a post office established in 1878. The Rio Grande Southern reached Placerville in 1890 and the town became an important livestock shipping point on the railroad. The business district of Placerville includes several historic structures and is located immediately northwest of the San Juan Skyway, Highway 145.

Many historic structures, such as this hay barn on the Dolores River are found on private property. Please respect private property and do not trespass. (Courtesy, San Juan National Forest)

Half a mile (.8 km) west of Placerville the Skyway intersects with Highway 62 where Leopard Creek flows into the San Miguel River. Here the Skyway leaves Highway 145 and follows Highway 62 over the Dallas Divide to the town of Ridgway in the Uncompahgre River Valley.

47

Famous Faces
San Juan

(Courtesy, Center for Southwest Studies, Fort Lewis College)

Jack Dempsey

Jack Dempsey fought a ten round bout in Durango on October 7, 1915 in the Gem Theatre at 10th & Main downtown. Dempsey, Pacific Coast champion at the time, fought Andy Malloy, Rocky Mountain champ, and presumably won. Reserved seats for the fight were $2.00 each and general admission was $1.00.

(Courtesy, La Plata County Historical Society)

Olga Little

One of the only women packers and the last of a dying breed, she serviced the mines around La Plata Canyon using 20-40 pack burros loaded with food and supplies, and continued to operate until the 1930's. She was a surprise guest on a special Denver edition of Ralph Edward's "This is Your Life" program in 1958.

Butch Cassidy

Robert Leroy Parker, alias "Butch Cassidy" of the infamous Wild Bunch gang, robbed the San Miquel Valley Bank in Telluride on June 24, 1889. Leading the pursuit was bank owner L. L. Nunn, who built the world's first alternating current electrical generating station near Telluride.

(Courtesy, Telluride Historical Museum)

Otto Mears

Otto Mears, "Pathfinder of the San Juans," was a hero to early white settlers, who depended on his toll roads and railroads to link them to the world beyond the San Juan basin. To the Ute Indians however, he was a man who grew richer with every square mile of Ute territory that was taken from them.

(Courtesy, Colorado State Historical Society. Neg. #F1012)

kyway

(Courtesy, The Owl in Monument Canyon, H. Jackson Clark)

Buckskin Charlie
Buckskin Charlie, one of the last of the Ute Chiefs, became the leader of the Muache band of Utes and raided the eastern plains of New Mexico. He was held in such great esteem as an Indian leader that he was called to Washington D.C. by five different presidents seeking his advice on Indian affairs.

William Henry Jackson
Jackson, famed 19th century photographer, was instrumental in the creation of Yellowstone National Park. He came to the San Juan Country in 1874 and made the first photographs of the cliff dwellings at Mesa Verde. Jackson was later hired by Otto Mears to photograph the scenic beauty along what is now the San Juan Skyway.

(Courtesy, Denver Public Library)

FAMOUS FACES

Al Wetherill
He was one of the Wetherill brothers, who with a lot of help from local Utes, "discovered" the cliff dwellings at Mesa Verde setting off the first tourist boom along the San Juan Skyway. The Wetherills went on to lead expeditions to ruins throughout the Four Corners Country, including Chaco Canyon and Navajo National Monument at Kayenta.

(Courtesy, Center for Southwest Studies, Fort Lewis College)

(Courtesy, Denver Public Library)

Francis Snowden
Snowden was a founder of Silverton in 1874 and built the first cabin in town, where a street still bears his name, as well as a 13,077 ft peak at Molas Pass along the San Juan Skyway. Snowden was an early mayor of Silverton which quickly became the central mining town of the San Juan Mountains.

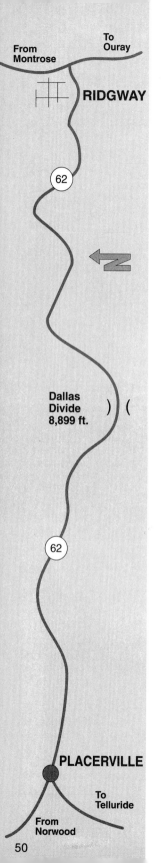

From
Montrose

To
Ouray

RIDGWAY

62

N

Dallas
Divide
8,899 ft.

) (

62

PLACERVILLE

To
Telluride

From
Norwood

PLACERVILLE TO RIDGWAY

Traveling northeast, up Leopard Creek, on the San Juan Skyway, Highway 62, you will very closely parallel the route of the Rio Grande Southern Railroad. Watch for remnants of the railbed and bridges as you climb the Dallas Divide. In the 13 miles (20.8 km) between the mouth of Leopard Creek and the summit of Dallas Divide, the railroad climbed more than 1,600 feet in elevation.

At the summit of Dallas Divide, elevation 8,989 feet, there is room to pull off the highway and take time to survey the Uncompahgre Valley to the northeast and the soaring summits of the San Juan Mountains to the south and east. The ragged, cathedral like peak to the southeast is Mount Sneffels, 14,150 feet

Placerville, 1887. (Courtesy, Colorado Historical Society. Neg. # F5478)

in elevation. The summit of Dallas Divide was an important loading point for livestock being shipped to distant markets or winter ranges.

Near Ridgway. (Courtesy, Colorado Historical Society. Neg. # F31004)

From the summit of Dallas Divide the Skyway descends 10.4 miles (16.6 km) to the town of Ridgway. You will travel past historic ranches tucked up against the foot of the towering San Juan Mountains. The community of Ridgway, like Dolores and Durango, began as a railroad town.

The Denver & Rio Grande Railroad was a major investor in the Rio Grande Southern Railroad, chartered in 1889. Mears and Denver and Rio Grande stockholders bought land and laid out the townsite of Ridgway in 1890. The new town would serve as Rio Grande Southern headquarters. The town was named for R. M. Ridgway, superintendent of the railroad and the man who supervised its construction. The Rio Grande Southern was completed in 1891. Mears' fortunes soared and Ridgway quickly took on an air of prosperous permanence. The older town of Dallas, two and a half miles down the Uncompahgre River, was abandoned as its residents moved upstream to the new town. Dave Wood, whose freighting company was headquartered in Dallas, went out of business. Rails had replaced the old wagon roads.

(Courtesy, La Plata County Historical Society)

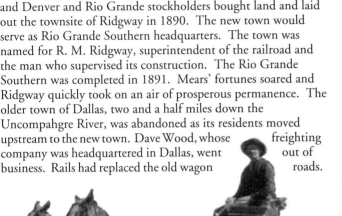

51

RIDGWAY

The Sherman Silver Purchasing Act of 1890 required the federal government to spend tens of millions of dollars a year to purchase the silver being produced in the United States, much of that silver coming from the San Juan Country. The completion of the Rio Grande Southern resulted in enormous increases in the mining of silver ore from the mines near Telluride and Rico. For Ridgway, 1892 was a very good year....

For much of America, 1892 was not a good year. Spiraling inflation was causing a recession. Banks, retail firms, and farms began going out of business. It was an election year. Presidential candidate Grover Cleveland voiced the concerns of wealthy financiers that government purchases of silver were fueling the inflation. Cleveland won the election and, in 1893, the Sherman Silver Purchasing Act was repealed.

The last stagecoach from Montrose to Ouray, August 23, 1887. (Courtesy, San Juan County Historical Society.)

Last day of the season for a Forest Service range reconnaissance crew in 1920. (Courtesy, San Juan National Forest)

Silver prices plunged and scores of silver mines throughout the San Juan Country closed overnight. Thousands of miners and their families, followed by businessmen, left the mountain towns. The Rio Grande Southern went into receivership, supervised by its largest investor, the Denver and Rio Grande Railroad. Mining in the San Juan Country would never again reach the levels enjoyed when silver was king. The Rio Grande Southern survived until 1951.

In 1893, Otto Mears lost control of his greatest achievement, the Rio Grande Southern, and he lost much of his wealth in the same year. But his influence on life in the San Juan Country continued. With silver nearly worthless, mining investors in the San Juan Country began paying more attention to the flecks of gold and the veins of lead and copper found in the San Juans. And, in Ridgway, the surviving businessmen began paying more attention to the livestock industry that surrounded their town. Ranching kept Ridgway alive. Today it is also a gateway to the recreation pleasures of the northern San Juan Country. Several historic structures are on streets north of Highway 62. The Rio Grande Southern depot is now a private residence.

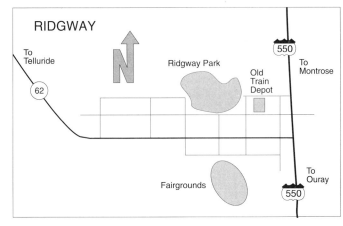

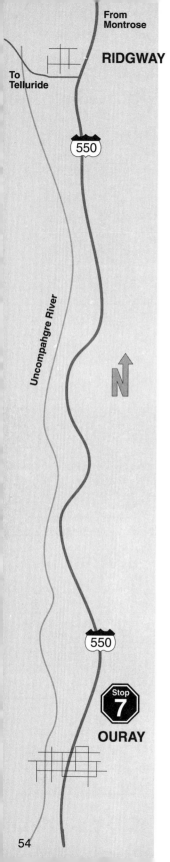

550

Uncompahgre River

N

550

Stop
7
OURAY

RIDGWAY TO OURAY

At Ridgway, which survived the traumas of 1893, the San Juan Skyway leaves Highway 162 and turns south on Highway 550 toward the upper reaches of the spectacular Uncompahgre River Valley. This is a good place to turn the calendar back to 1868 and the history of the Utes for whom this was once an undisputed homeland. The Treaty of 1868 had reduced the once vast Ute homeland to the part of Colorado lying west of the Continental Divide including the San Juan Country. By 1870, prospectors were trespassing in the high valleys, mining bits of the richest ores, and hauling them out by burro trains. Coloradoans began demanding the opening of the San Juan Country to settlement. The Utes resisted. The Brunot Agreement of 1873 turned the mountain tops over to the miners and preserved the valleys and lower elevations for the Utes.

In 1875, a new Indian agency was located on the Uncompahgre River near Colona a few miles north of Ridgway. Farther north, on the outskirts of present-day Montrose, Ouray, and his revered and influential wife Chipeta, were given a farm. Additional agencies were located on the White River in north-western Colorado and at present-day Ignacio, on the Pine River southeast of Durango.

Chief Ouray relied heavily on his wife Chipeta's advice in negotiating with the government. She left Colorado, with most of the Utes, after his death. (Courtesy, Colorado Historical Society, Neg.#F1012)

Utes crossing the Pine River near Ignacio, 1899. (Courtesy, Colorado Historical Society. Neg. # F82)

Because of his role in persuading the Utes to accept the terms of the agreements of 1868 and 1873, Ouray was accorded the status of hero among the white citizens of Colorado Territory. Mears, because of his role in mediating treaty negotiations, won equal fame and acclaim.

But the Treaty of 1868 and the 1873 agreement did little to satisfy those who wanted even more Ute territory opened to settlement. Demands grew for the complete removal of the Utes from Colorado. Flagrant trespassing on Ute territory continued. Ouray was under increasing suspicion and pressure from his own people, who believed he was selling out their interests. Colorado leaders increased pressure on Ouray to persuade the Utes to leave Colorado. Ouray himself was increasingly disillusioned with federal and state leaders who did not keep the promises made in the treaties and agreements.

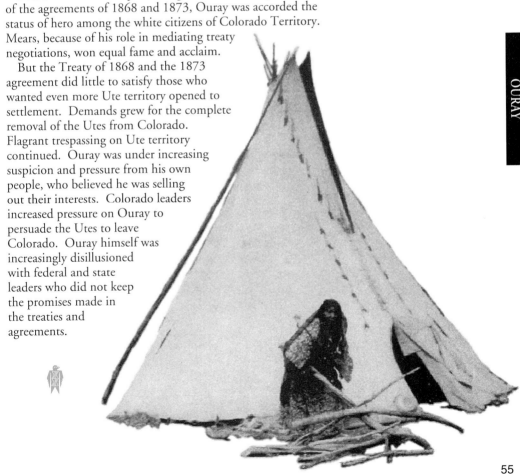

The Ouray to Silverton Toll Road went up this canyon where the San Juan Skyway goes today. (Courtesy, Colorado Historical Society. Neg. # F36402)

RIDGWAY TO OURAY

In 1879, Ute anger over continuing trespassing and government policies erupted into armed resistance. The White River Indian Agent Nathan Meeker and several of his staff were killed in one incident and several calvarymen killed in another. That provided the excuse needed to remove the Utes from Colorado. In 1880, federal legislation was enacted which provided for the removal of the Utes. That legislation stated that the removal must be agreed to by three quarters of all Ute males over eighteen. Ouray, ill and depressed over what was happening to his people, began the difficult process of trying to convince the Utes to agree to move to Utah. He died before achieving that goal.

Otto Mears began paying Ute males to sign the agreement to leave Colorado. It is doubtful he ever got nearly the required three quarters of Ute males to sign, but the agreement was enforced. In 1881, the Utes, Chipeta with them, were moved

Utah. A few were allowed to stay in what are now the Southern Ute and Ute Mountain Ute Reservations, a short, thin strip of land along the southern border of Colorado. Their descendants are there today.

Whether Chief Ouray was a pragmatist who feared total genocide if his people resisted white pressure or a traitor to the cause of his own people will remain forever unknown. Whether Mears was a friend of all the Utes or in conspiracy with Ouray for his own enrichment, will remain equally unknown. Mears certainly profited from each successive reduction of Ute territory. The two men are forever linked in the history of the San Juan Country. No two men since have had an equal impact on events in the region. The town of Ouray is named in honor of the Ute chief.

A newspaper advertisement expressing anti-Ute sentiment. (Courtesy, Colorado Historical Society. Neg. # F44177)

The Utes leaving Colorado, 1881. (Courtesy, Colorado Historical Society. Neg. # 15557)

"Ouray is - what shall I say? The prettiest mountain town in Colorado? That wouldn't do. A dozen other places would deny it, and the cynics who never saw anything different from a rough camp of cabins in some quartz gulch, would sneer that this is faint praise. Yet that it is among the most attractive in situation, in climate, in appearance, and in the society it affords, there can be no doubt. There are few western villages that can boast so much civilization."

THE CREST OF THE CONTINENT
Ernest Ingersoll, 1885

Coach on the Ouray to Silverton Toll Road, now the San Juan Skyway. (Courtesy, Colorado Historical Society. Neg. #F15140)

OURAY

Ouray was granted a post office in 1875, among the earliest in the San Juan Mountains. The community grew slowly as silver mines opened in the canyons leading into town. Growth quickened with the coming of the Denver & Rio Grande Railroad from the north in late 1887. Ouray County built a segment of road south up the

Ouray in the 1890s. (Courtesy, Colorado Historical Society. Neg. # F229)

Uncompahgre Canyon which was incorporated by Otto Mears into his most famous toll road, from Silverton to Ouray, completed in 1883. That toll road ultimately connected a Denver & Rio Grande Railroad terminus in Ouray to a terminus of the same railroad in Silverton, thus lowering the cost of transporting ores from mining camps in the mountainous terrain between the two towns.

Ouray, like all of the mining towns of the San Juan Country, suffered from repeal of the Sherman Silver Purchasing Act in 1893. But, as elsewhere, mining investors quickly turned their attention to gold. In 1896, Thomas Walsh, an Irish immigrant, acquired and expanded what is perhaps one of the most famous gold mines in Colorado, the Camp Bird Mine located on Canyon Creek above Ouray. After the Camp Bird had produced more than $2,500,000 in gold, Walsh sold it to a British syndicate in 1902 for $5,200,000. The Camp Bird produced another $22,000,000 in gold over the next fifteen years and continued producing on a lesser scale for many years thereafter.

Unlike many San Juan mining towns, Ouray was a tourist destination from the time of its founding. The spectacular location, the relatively low elevation, and the hot springs combined to make it a mecca for city dwellers eager for rest and recreation. Today it is a starting point for four wheel drive roads that follow historic pack and wagon roads. Take time to wander through Ouray looking at its many fine Victorian buildings ... some of which are actually late twentieth century architecture faithfully replicating the style so popular a century ago.

Spring snowstorm on Red Mountain Pass. (Courtesy, San Juan County Historical Society)

THE OURAY COUNTY MUSEUM

The Ouray County Museum is located in the original Ouray Hospital built in 1887 and includes three floors of Ouray County history. It is open seven days a week from May 1 through October 15 and Friday, Saturday, and Sunday the remainder of the year. Exhibits feature pioneer days, mining history, Indian history, photographs, and hospital memorabilia. Two historic log cabins are located on the grounds. There are evening programs weekly from late June through August. A walking tour map of Ouray is available. Hours from May 1 to June 15 and September 1 to October 15 are 10 a.m. to 4 p.m., Monday through Saturday, and 1 p.m. to 4 p.m. on Sunday. Hours from June 16 to August 31 are 9 a.m. to 6 p.m. Monday through Friday, 9 a.m. to 5 p.m. Saturday, and 1 p.m. to 5 p.m. Sunday. From October 16 through April 30, the Museum is open Friday, Saturday, and Sunday from 1 p.m. to 4 p.m. Admission is $3 for adults and $1 for children. Proceeds benefit the Ouray County Historical Society.

7,706 feet above sea level.

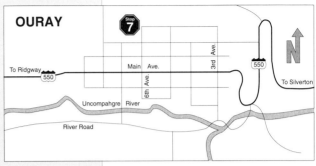

OURAY

To Ridgway 550 — Main Ave. — 3rd Ave. — 550 To Silverton
6th Ave.
Uncompahgre River
River Road

(Courtesy, La Plata County Historical Society)

Pack train hauling iron rails, Ouray. (Courtesy, Colorado Historical Society. Neg. # F3013 photograph by F.S. Bolster)

OURAY

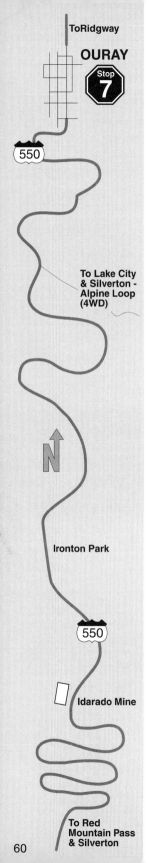

To Ridgway

OURAY

Stop 7

550

To Lake City
& Silverton -
Alpine Loop
(4WD)

N

Ironton Park

550

Idarado Mine

To Red
Mountain Pass
& Silverton

OURAY TO IRONTON

The six and one-half miles (10.4 km) of the San Juan Skyway south of Ouray is one of the most breathtaking stretches of mountain road in the nation. The Skyway is built on top of Mears' Ouray to Silverton toll road. Two and -three-quarters miles (4-4 km) south of Ouray there is a fenced pullout, the Bear Creek Falls overlook, on the west side of the road. This a good place to stop and ponder the work of Otto Mears. A monument of him is on the east side of the highway at the top of the falls. The Skyway crosses the top of Bear Creek Falls on a modern concrete bridge. The toll road crossed in the same place on a high, narrow wooden bridge. The toll gate was located at the upper end of the bridge. There was no way to sneak around the gatekeeper. The price for a horse and rider was $.50. A horse-drawn wagon got through for $5. Because there was no other route between the mountain mining camps and Ouray, the gatekeeper was the central news and gossip source on what was happening on the upper and lower stretches of the road.

The Schoolhouse at the Camp Bird Miine near Ouray. (Courtesy, Colorado Historical Society. Neg. # F33392)

Otto Mears' tollgate at the top of Bear Creek Falls, on the Ouray to Silverton toll road. (Courtesy, Center for Southwest Studies, Fort Lewis College)

A mile (1.6 km) farther south, up the canyon, the Skyway passes the mouth of Poughkeepsie Gulch. A four-wheel drive road leads up Poughkeepsie Gulch to the four-wheel drive Alpine Loop which follows a network of pack trails and wagon roads over spectacular mountain passes connecting Silverton and Lake City.

Two-and-a-half miles (4 km) farther south the Skyway passes through a concrete avalanche shed, built to protect winter travelers from the deadly East Riverside Slide. Across the canyon is the chute of the West Riverside Slide. When the two avalanches run in the same winter, the canyon can fill with snow and debris up to the foundations of the snowshed itself.

Snow Tunnel through an avalanche on the Ouray to Silverton Toll Road. (Courtesy, Colorado Historical Society. Neg. # F2787)

The Riverside Slide on Red Mountain Pass, now part of the San Juan Skyway, on July 6, 1888. A snowshed now covers the highway in this avalanche path. (courtesy, Colorado Historical Society. Neg. # F2504 photograph by Chas Goodman, Montrose, Colorado)

AVALANCHES

Avalanches gaining speed down thousands of feet of mountainside not only remove everything in their paths down to the bare rock, but they create concussion waves that can destroy nearby structures left untouched by the plunging snow itself. Certain types of avalanches compact snow with cement-like hardness on highways and canyon bottoms. Avalanche paths or chutes are treeless ribbons running down the face of mountains. There are hundreds of avalanche paths, many of them named, in the San Juan Country. Some of the most famous are visible between Ouray and Silverton on the San Juan Skyway. Watch for avalanche paths as you travel over Red Mountain Pass.

BEAR CREEK FALLS

IRONTON PARK TO IDARADO MINE

A quarter mile south (.4 km) of the East Riverside Slide snowshed is a memorial to the people who have died in that slide since 1963. In the century between 1875 and 1975, 95 people died in avalanches in San Juan County alone, most of them while scores of mining camps and hundreds of mines and boarding houses still dotted the high country. Today avalanche control techniques and the practice of closing passes in peak avalanche times have greatly reduced avalanche deaths. Skiers venturing into slide-prone areas now account for most avalanche fatalities in the San Juan high country.

By 1892, all of the surviving towns on the San Juan Skyway but Cortez were served by at least one of three railroads running over 245 miles of track. Two of those railroads—the Rio Grande Southern Railroad and the Silverton Railroad—with 190 miles of track, were built and run by Otto Mears. Mears dreamed of connecting Ouray and Silverton by rail. That he never did. The steep grades between Ouray and Ironton Park, the north end of which is about one mile (1.6 km) south of the East Riverside Slide memorial plaque, defied even the Pathfinder of the San Juans.

Traveling south through Ironton Park, a wide flat-bottomed valley that provides some relief from the winding road toward the summit of Red Mountain Pass, you will notice what little remains of the mining camps of Albany and Ironton spread along the banks of Red Mountain Creek. The tracks of the Silverton Railroad reached Albany in 1889 and stopped where Red Mountain Creek abruptly plunges over the lip of Ironton Park into the Uncompahgre Canyon.

The Silverton Railroad traversed the east slope of the valley on a grade so steep and around a switch back so sharp that the covered Corkscrew Gulch Turntable was constructed to turn the engine in order to continue the journey up or down the grade.

Underground at the Camp Bird Miine near Ouray. (Courtesy, Colorado Historical Society. Neg. # F3106

Riding the Camp Bird Tram. (Courtesy, Colorado Historical Society. Neg. # F7655)

In the 1890's, Red Mountain Town was a booming mining camp served by the Silverton Railroad. (Courtesy, Center for Southwest Studies, Fort Lewis College)

At the south end of Ironton Park, the Skyway begins the final climb around numerous hairpin turns toward the summit of Red Mountain Pass. A mile (1.6 km) above the first switchbacks mining structures seen across the canyon on the slope of Red Mountain, are what remains of the mining camp of Guston and the Yankee Girl, Robinson, and Genesse-Vanderbilt mines.

The turntable on the Silverton Railroad, Red Mountain Pass. (Courtesy, Center for Southwest Studies, Fort Lewis College.)

) (

550

N

550

Stop
8

SILVERTON

To Durango

Red Mountain Pass to Silverton

Two more miles (3.2 km) up the pass the Skyway passes the Idarado Mine. There is space here to pull off the road and look at a modern mining operation that continued into the 1970s. The tunnels leading in from the Idarado are connected with those leading in from Pandora, just two miles from Telluride. Trespassing off the highway right-of-way-way is not permitted. This is a good place, to contemplate the three iron-rich peaks towering into the eastern sky from which Red Mountain Pass got its name.

(Courtesy, Colorado Historical Society. Neg. # F31696)

Two miles (3.2 km) farther south on the Skyway, thirteen and one-half miles (21.6 km) south of Ouray at the summit of Red Mountain Pass, is the highest point on the San Juan Skyway, 11,018 feet above sea level. The historic structures on the east side of the summit are on private property. The mining camp of Red Mountain Town was located just north of the summit. Little evidence of its existence remains today.

From the summit of Red Mountain Pass, the San Juan Skyway drops steeply into the Mineral Creek drainage, following the challenging seven percent grade once followed by the Silverton Railroad. Two and one-half miles (4 km) south of the summit is Chattanooga Curve.

Red Mountain Town at the summit of Red Mountain Pass. Souvenir seekers and other vandals have destroyed almost all traces of this community. (Courtesy, Colorado Historical Society. Neg. # F34276)

The Yankee Girl Mine on Red Mountain Pass. (Courtesy, Colorado Historical Society. Neg. # 3772 photograph by Adams, Silverton, Colorado)

A few remnants of the mining camp of Chattanooga, on the banks of Mineral Creek, can still be seen just south of the curve.

The Skyway follows the canyons of Mineral Creek until suddenly, 24 miles (38.4 km) south of Ouray, the canyon opens into the flat, mountain-rimmed expanse known as Baker's Park. The mining history—thus, the modern history—of the San Juan Country began in Baker's Park in 1860 and the mining industry continued here until 1991, longer than anywhere else in the San Juan Mountains.

The Silverton to Ouray Stage in Silverton. (Courtesy, Colorado Historical Society. Neg. # F14976)

"Outcroppings and large deposits of iron ore are found in Baker's Park, and blue carbonates of lime on Sultan Mountain. The first mine worked to any extent was the Little Giant, discovered in 1870, located in Arrastra Gulch. The smelter run of the ores treated from mines in this district, in 1877, varied from $150 to $2,000 per ton...

Silverton is the principal town in the district. From this point, most of the miners from the La Plata and Uncompahgre districts obtain their supplies. It lies in Baker's Park, one of the loveliest bits of nature, hidden away in the mountains, and is destined to be a town of no small importance in the near future."

"History of Colorado"
W.B. Vickers in **HISTORY OF THE ARKANSAS VALLEY, COLORADO, 1881**

Silverton

The Animas River, named by early Spaniards El Rio de las Animas Perdidas, The River of Lost Souls, flows into Baker's Park from the north. There it is joined by Cement Creek flowing into Baker's Park from the northwest and by Mineral Creek, entering from the west. Less than five miles up the river from the town of Silverton, Cunningham Gulch empties into the Animas River from the east. The Animas River flows south from Baker's Park through a narrow canyon toward Durango. The creeks and canyons provided access through and over the fortress of peaks surrounding Baker's Park.

Charles Baker and a handful of men entered Baker's Park in 1860 in search of gold dust in the sand and gravel bars of the Animas River and tributary creeks. They found some of what they were looking for and the news spread quickly. By the autumn of 1860 hundreds--by some accounts, thousands--of prospectors were heading for the heart of the San Juan Country deep inside Ute territory. Winter forced them out of Baker's Park or delayed their approach. A small

STOP 8 - SILVERTON

THE SAN JUAN COUNTY MUSEUM

The San Juan County Museum is located on the north end of Greene Street, Silverton's main street, next to the county courthouse. The museum, established in 1964, is open from May to mid-October. It is housed in the former San Juan County jail and includes a variety of indoor and outdoor exhibits depicting the history of Silverton and nearby mining camps. It includes a gift shop and bookstore. Museum hours are from 9 a.m. to 5 p.m. daily through mid-September and 10 a.m. to 3 p.m. through mid-October. Admission is $1.50 for all visitors over 12, children under 12 are admitted free. Proceeds go to the non-profit San Juan County Historical Society preserving the history of San Juan County.

Elevation 9,320 feet above sea level.

Red Mountain Brass Band, Red Mountain Town. (Courtesy, Colorado Historical Society. Neg. # F31696)

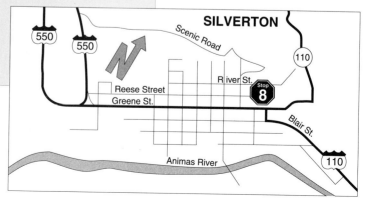

The man gesturing in this photograph is Ernest Ingersoll who wrote extensively about the San Juan country. (Courtesy, Center for Southwest Studies, Fort Lewis College)

army of prospectors, a few with brides or families, gathered in a hastily built village of log cabins at the mouth of the Animas Canyon 25 miles south of Baker's Park to await the spring of 1861.

It was a short-lived gold rush. Inaccessibility, Utes anger over the trespassers, a harsh winter, and disappointing prospecting results combined to drive the prospectors out. By the end of 1861 the San Juan Country was empty of prospectors and securely back in the hands of the Utes. The Civil War, the Utes, and inaccessibility combined to keep it that way for another decade. But the gold panned by Baker and his party was not forgotten.

The Gold King tramway and mine near Silverton. (Courtesy, Colorado Historical Society. Neg. # F23297)

A parade down Greene Street in Silverton. (Courtesy, Colorado Historical Society. neg. # 42576)

SILVERTON

By 1870, prospectors were crossing Stony Pass from the Rio Grande River east of the Continental Divide, descending into Cunningham Gulch, and spreading out along the Animas in violation of the Treaty of 1868. A cluster of log cabins, known as Howardsville, grew up at the mouth of Cunningham Gulch.

The Brunot Agreement of 1873 with the Utes gave the prospectors what they wanted, the mountain tops of the San Juan Country. The rush was on in earnest. The town site of what is now Silverton was laid out in 1874, and a post office established there in 1875. The new town in Baker's Park soon became the mining center of the San Juan Country. The proliferation of producing mines along the Animas River attracted the attention of railroad companies headquartered in Denver. The companies raced one another to be the first to reach the San Juans. The Denver & Rio Grande Railroad won the contest and the first D&RG train from the new railroad town of Durango rolled into Baker's Park in July, 1882.

Silverton panorama from Kendall Mountain in 1912. (Courtesy, Center for Sourthwest Studies, Fort Lewis College)

Silverton, like all the Victorian era mining towns of the San Juan Country, had within its town limits and in the surrounding high country camps and boarding houses a far greater supply of bachelors than of brides. Saloons, gambling houses, dance halls, and houses of prostitution provided a Saturday night alternative to the miners who didn't have a wife and a warm fire to go home to. Such nightlife was tolerated—barely—by the respectable citizens of the mining towns but it was limited to a designated area of town, the red light district. Prostitutes—often referred to as "ladies of the evening" in the newspapers of the time—were not welcome in the proper neighborhoods and were ostracized by all of polite society.

The Silverton Cowboy band. (Courtesy, Colorado Historical Society. Neg. #F42574 photograph by "Dad Covey")

Neither did proper ladies from proper neighborhoods venture into red light districts unless armed with Temperance Union axes for the purpose of smashing bars.

Propriety, and an increasing supply of civilizing brides, eventually won out and the red light districts vanished. In Silverton, the red light district was spread along a few blocks of Blair Street. In Silverton the demise of the red light district seemed almost to trigger a lingering fond memory that lasted for decades. Maybe there was more fun to be had on Blair Street than at the dramatic readings staged in the formal parlors on Reese Street....

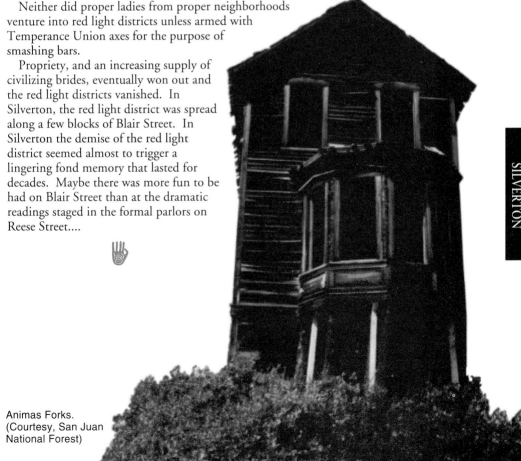

Animas Forks.
(Courtesy, San Juan
National Forest)

The daily passenger train of the Silverton Northern at Eureka in 1906. (Courtesy, Center for Southwest Studies, Fort Lewis College)

As time went on the industrial revolution caught up with mining in the San Juan Country. Mining and milling became increasingly mechanized. Where once thousands of miners and millworkers were required to produce ore and concentrates, by the mid-twentieth century a few dozen miners and millworkers could maintain the same level of production. Even in the best of times, the great booms of the San Juans were a thing of the past.

The last decades of the nineteenth century were a time when an expanding, industrializing United States could not meet the demand for laborers in the mountain mines and mills.

Hispanics from northern New Mexico, descendants of the first Europeans to enter the San Juan Country centuries before, came to work in the mines. Thousands of immigrant laborers from Ireland, Wales, Cornwall, Scandinavia, Poland, China, and Italy streamed in to work in the mines and build the railroads. They saved their pay and sent home for their families. Silverton, Rico, Ouray, and Telluride became multi-lingual, multi-cultural communities with a unique cosmopolitan air of their own.

The first automobile to reach Silverton, August, 1910. (Courtesy, San Juan County Historical Society)

Despite the fact that heroes such as Otto Mears, a Russian immigrant, and the Camp Bird's Thomas Walsh, an Irish immigrant, fueled the fortunes of the region's Anglo-American elite, ethnic prejudice ruled the day. Each immigrant culture formed a community of its own within the larger towns. But, when they could afford to leave for big cities or when times got bad, the elite packed up and went elsewhere. The immigrants stayed and worked the mines. They saved their money and bought Main Street.

Gold ore continued to flow from the portal at Gladstone for trucking to the mill at the upper end of Baker's Park until July, 1991. The 1991 closure of the mine and mill may have marked the end of mining in the San Juan Mountains for decades or centuries to come. Silverton today is a monument to its longlived and very recent mining past. Its citizens are determined to preserve the remnants of the mining era which surround the town. Silverton's future may well be as the place where the world comes to see and to understand the mining history—thus, the foundation of the modern history—of the San Juan Country.

The toll house on the Champion cliffs with Silverton in the background. This photo was problably taken in 1907, after the toll house had closed. (Courtesy, San Juan County Historical Society.)

Denver & Rio Grande 2-8-0 Number 281 switching cars at the Silver Lake mill in 1903. (Courtesy, Center for Southwest Studies, Fort Lewis College)

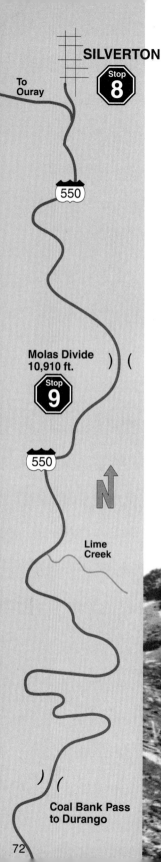

SILVERTON

To Ouray

Stop 8

550

Molas Divide 10,910 ft.

Stop 9

550

N

Lime Creek

Coal Bank Pass to Durango

SILVERTON AND MOLAS PASS

The Denver & Rio Grande Railroad between Durango and Silverton was sold in 1980 and is now known as the Durango and Silverton Narrow Gauge Railroad. As many as four trains a day make the 45-mile run between the two towns when the tracks are free of snow. The San Juan Skyway closely parallels former railroads along most of its way. However, for most of the distance between Durango and Silverton, the Skyway climbs over mountain passes while the trains follow the Animas River deep in the Animas Canyon.

From Silverton, follow the San Juan Skyway south, up the face of the Champion Cliffs, six and one-half miles (10.4 km) to the summit of Molas Pass, 10,910 feet above sea level.

Seventeen and one-half miles (28 km) south of the

Before the highway was built over Coalbank Hill, the road followed the Lime Creek Canyon. (Courtesy, La Plata County Historical Society)

SUMMIT OF MOLAS PASS

A United States Forest Service interpretive overlook at Molas Pass provides information about the landscape on both sides of the Skyway. To the east of the pass the rugged Grenadier Range is visible beyond the Animas Canyon. The forest here burned in 1879, and despite attempts at reforestation, the mostly treeless landscape provides mute evidence of the centuries required to replace forests at this elevation. This fire-scorched area is called the Lime Creek Burn. Elevation 10,910 feet.

Molas Pass, 1923, still barren after the Lime Creek Burn of 1879. (Courtesy, San Juan National Forest)

summit of Molas Pass is the summit of Coal Bank Hill. United States Forest Service rest facilities are located here. From the summit of Coal Bank Hill, the Skyway begins a steep, winding, southward descent to the Purgatory-Durango Ski Resort. South of Purgatory, the Skyway skirts the base of the towering Hermosa Cliffs then descends once more into the broad, fertile Animas River Valley north of Durango. The San Juan Skyway parallels the Durango & Silverton Narrow Gauge Railroad tracks from here to Durango.

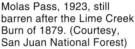

(Courtesy, La Plata County Historical Society)

MOLAS PASS

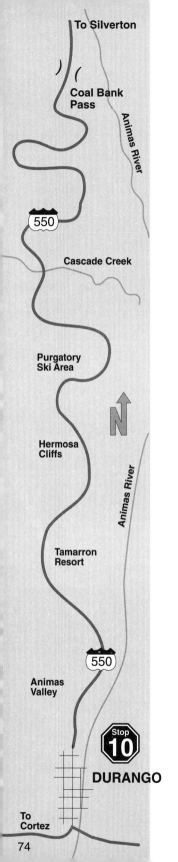

To Silverton

Coal Bank Pass

Animas River

550

Cascade Creek

Purgatory Ski Area

N

Hermosa Cliffs

Animas River

Tamarron Resort

550

Animas Valley

Stop 10

DURANGO

To Cortez

COAL BANK PASS - ANIMAS VALLEY

The first known permanent settlements in the Animas Valley appeared nearly 2,000 years ago when Puebloan farmers began to grow plots of corn to supplement the seasonal round. Puebloan farming continued in the valley for several centuries before the move to the mesa tops to the south and west.

Modern settlement of the Animas Valley, after the short-lived Animas City of 1860, began in 1875. Farms spread across the valley floor to feed the floods of prospectors rushing into Baker's Park up the river. In 1877 a second settlement called Animas City, now part of the northern end of Durango, was granted a post office. Animas City grew in anticipation of the arrival of a railroad that would link Denver to Silverton, passing through the young community on its way toward the mining camps in the mountains. The railroad would lend permanence to Animas City.

The builders of the new railroad had ideas of their own. In 1880 they bought land south of Animas City, laid out the town site of Durango, and built a depot, rail yards, and a roundhouse at the southern end of their own new town. Durango gained permanence with the arrival of the Denver and Rio Grande Railroad in 1881.

SKYWAY BICYCLING

Bicycling along the Skyway has always been popular, evidenced by the Durango Wheel Club photo on the opposite page. The mountains, the scenery, the beautiful valleys all combine to lure enthusiasts to this region to ride. Today, several major bicycling events take place annually, including the Iron Horse Classic where over a thousand cyclists race the narrow gauge train to Silverton (yes, the bicyclists always win) and sanctioned U.S. Cycling Federation races in Telluride. In addition every fall, the Bicycle Tour of the San Juans features a three day tour along the Skyway as the tree leaves are changing, involving citizen riders from across the United States. And then there's the "Death Ride," appropriately named by the bicyclists who endeavor to complete the entire Skyway loop in just one day. The record is 14 hours 25 minutes, think about that as you're driving up the grades and over the passes.

Durango's rapid transition from frontier camp to civilized regional center was due in part to the crusading woman, Caroline Romney, who ran one of its first newspapers, The Durango Record. Mrs. Romney, though ever the lady, never backed down from a fight.

ANIMAS VALLEY

Looking north towards Hermosa on the West Animas Road in the 1920's before private development of the Animas Valley north of Durango. (Courtesy, San Juan National Forest)

Trimble Hot Springs has attracted visitors for decades and does today. The hotel shown here no longer stands. (Courtesy, Trimble Hot Springs)

DURANGO

The journalist Ernest Ingersoll described a visit to Durango in 1883. The description still holds:

Early Durango. (Courtesy, La Plata County Historical Society)

"Durango is beautifully located on the eastern bank of the river, the commercial portion being on the first or lower bench, and the residences on the second or higher plateau. Thus the homes of the people occupy a sightly position, apart from the turmoil of traffic, while lofty mountains and wall-like cliffs shelter the valley on all sides...Here centers the business whose operations extend throughout the entire mountain system, and the tillage and stock-raising districts of northwestern New Mexico. The great supply stores, with their heavy assortments of general merchandise, indicate a jobbing trade of no mean dimensions, and one which is steadily growing; while the extensive and elegant retail shops, unsurpassed in the state outside of Denver, bear evidence of the refined demands and prosperity of the citizens. Here also are concentrated the social, religious, and school advantages which make up an intellectual nucleus."

Ernest Ingersoll,
1885 THE CREST OF THE CONTINENT

A street car in Durango. (Courtesy, Colorado Historical Society) Neg. # F31857

The smelters, casting a pall of black coal smoke across the sky that was seen as a sign of industrial progress, are gone now. The trainloads of ore coming to the Durango smelters or passing through Durango to more distant smelters are things of the past. But unlike her neighbors, Durango's prosperity and future was never tied to a single commodity, whether it be metals, timber, energy, tourism, livestock, or crops. Durango possessed a diverse economy that rode out the economic panics that took such great tolls on single economy towns in the region.

THE ANIMAS MUSEUM

The Animas Museum, run by the La Plata County Historical Society, is housed in a historic schoolhouse in north Durango at the corner of 31st Street and West Second Avenue. It is open May through September and features exhibits on local history, Indian cultures, and western history. A turn-of-the-century classroom serves as an exhibit of early educational methods and materials. Programs include lectures and slide shows. The Animas Museum is open from 10 a.m. to 6 p.m. Monday through Saturday. Admission is $1.75 and children under 12 are admitted free. Proceeds fund the work of the La Plata County Historical Society.

Elevation 6,523 feet above sea level.

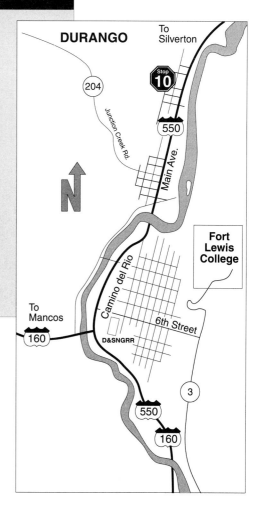

DURANGO

To Silverton

Stop 10

204

Junction Creek Rd.

550

Main Ave.

N

To Mancos

160

Camino del Rio

D&SNGRR

Fort Lewis College

6th Street

550

160

3

(Courtesy, Center for Southwest Studies, Fort Lewis College)

Schoolhouse in Animas City, now north Durango, in 1904. (Courtesy Colorado Historical Society. Neg. # F36417

DURANGO

David Dwyer was a pioneer settler in La Plata County and one of its early sheriffs. (Courtesy, La Plata County Historical Society)

Fine brick homes replaced the first log cabins in Animas City, now part of Durango. (Courtesy, La Plata County Historical Society)

(Courtesy, La Plata County Historical Society)

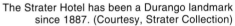

The Strater Hotel has been a Durango landmark since 1887. (Courtesy, Strater Collection)

Durango quickly became a mercantile center for the vast Four Corners country. (Courtesy, La Plata County Historical Society)

Begin the Adventure of a Lifetime

Colorado's Campus in the Sky

Fort Lewis College, Durango campus, est. 1956, now shown, 1994.

Founded as a military fort in 1878 near Pagosa Springs, Fort Lewis was moved to its Hesperus location in 1880 to be closer to the growing pioneer settlement of Animas City (now north Durango). The U.S. government abandoned the site as a military post in 1891, and in its stead, established a school offering free education to Native American students.

Fort Lewis became a state high school of agriculture in 1911 and evolved into a junior college by the late 1940s. Fort Lewis moved to its Durango campus in 1956 with the goal of establishing a four-year undergraduate liberal arts college. The first

Fort Lewis, 1885.

baccalaureate degrees were granted in 1964. Today, more than 4,270 students from throughout the United States and the world attend Fort Lewis College.

Fort Lewis still maintains much of that adventurous spirit in its programs and faculty, many of whom are recognized regionally and nationally for their pioneering work in teaching, research and community service.

Fort Lewis College students work side by side with their professors exploring solutions to a wilderness management problem, investigating a marketing issue for a local business or examining the motivations of the human spirit. The adventure is limited only by imagination, curiosity and creativity.

Chemistry classroom, Old Fort Lewis campus, 1920's

Students looking for an intellectual challenge will find the adventure of a lifetime at Fort Lewis College.

A college education should be the start of a lifelong adventure of learning and living. And if you're a little more adventurous than most, are curious about the world around you and enjoy a challenge now and then, you're the kind of student we're looking for at Fort Lewis College.

We offer 24 exciting liberal arts degree programs uniquely flavored by the history, cultures and environment of Southwest Colorado. Here you can explore the limits of your imagination on a campus tucked in the shadows of the rugged La Plata Mountains.

Fort Lewis College's story is rooted in the adventure of settling a new land and exploring the boundaries of spirit and intellect. In fact, Fort Lewis' namesake played a key role in the settlement and development along the San Juan Skyway.

FT. LEWIS COLLEGE

FORT LEWIS COLLEGE

For more information about
Fort Lewis College, call or write:

Office of Admission and Development
Fort Lewis College • 1000 Rim Drive
Durango, Colorado 81301-3999 • 303-247-7184

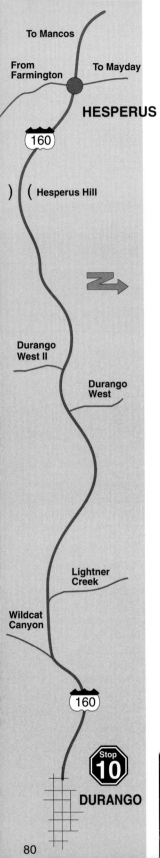

To Mancos

From Farmington

To Mayday

HESPERUS

160

) (Hesperus Hill

Durango
West II

Durango
West

Lightner
Creek

Wildcat
Canyon

160

Stop
10

DURANGO

Durango to Hesperus

In Durango the San Juan Skyway leaves Highway 550 and turns west, up Lightner Creek Canyon, toward Hesperus, Mancos, and Cortez. The canyons immediately west of Durango were the source of coal to fuel the town's smelters and the area's railroads. For a decade that coal came down Lightner Creek Canyon in wagon. In 1890, construction of the Rio Grand Southern Railroad began simultaneously in Durango and Ridgway with both sets of crews scheduled to meet in Rico, completing the 162 mile arc between the two towns. From Durango the Rio Grande Southern construction crews headed up Wildcat Canyon toward Hesperus. The coal wagons vanished, rail branches were built to the coal mines, and the coal industry flourished. The roadbed of one of the coal lines is still visible today ascending the slopes of the Twin Buttes one mile west of Durango.

At Hesperus, eleven miles (17.6 km) west of Durango, the

Olga Little's pack train supplied mines in the La Plata Mountains well into the twentieth century. (Courtesy, La Plata County Historical Society)

valley of the La Plata River cuts through the shallow coal beds which are visible on a hillside just south of the Skyway.

North of Hesperus the mouth of La Plata Canyon can be seen where it opens into the broader valley. That is the site of the mining camp of Mayday, gateway into the mineral districts of the La Plata Mountains, which like the coal mines, benefited by the arrival of the Rio Grande Southern. Mayday was headquarters for Olga Little and her pack animals which carried ore from mountain mines to the railhead there. El Sierra de la Plata, the Silver Mountains, was named by Spaniards long before the coming of the railroad.

Hesperus is at the north end of Highway 140 which goes to Farmington, New Mexico.

Highway 140 passes the old Fort Lewis Military Post and college campus, now a Colorado State University Agricultural Experiment Station, a few miles south of Hesperus.

Durango has been a multi-cultural community since its founding. (Courtesy, Center for Southwest Studies, Fort Lewis College)

HESPERUS TO MANCOS

For two and one-half miles (4 km) west from Hesperus the roadbed of the Rio Grande Southern closely parallels the Skyway and, at times, can be seen along the highway right-of-way on the north side of the road. The Rio Grande Southern then veered to the north to begin climbing the final ridge before descending into the Mancos River Valley. Three miles west (4.8 km) of Hesperus, the Skyway begins descending into Cherry Creek Valley and Thompson Park, passing a monument to the Dominguez-Escalante Expedition of 1776 and historic ranches along the way. The

Mancos looking south, 1893. (Courtesy, Colorado Historical Society Neg. # F24252)

road curves south and climbs Mancos Hill then descends into the Mancos River Valley to rejoin the route of Rio Grande Southern in the town of Mancos sixteen and one-half miles (26.4 km) west of Hesperus.

El Rio Mancos was named by Spanish explorers in the eighteenth century. Mancos means "Crippled One" and local legend has it that a member of an exploration party suffered an injury here, thus the name El Rio Mancos. Dominating the Valley on the west is the sheer face of Mesa Verde, meaning "Green Table". The spectacular cliff dwellings in

Hispanic woman wearing a handmade Spanish lace shawl. (Courtesy, Colorado Historical Society. Neg.# F41269)

Mesa Verde National Park re on Mesa Verde.

The ancient Indian trail through the Mancos Valley and skirting Mesa Verde was the route followed by the earliest Spaniards and eventually became the Spanish Trail leading west from Santa Fe and veering north through Ute Territory to avoid the Navajos south of the San Juan River. Though Spain lost the San Juan Country to Mexico in 1821 and Mexico ceded it to the United States in 1848, the Spanish placenames are a reminder of the centuries-old Hispanic influence on the region. That influence, and the contribution of Hispanics, continues today.

Merchant George Bauer's mansion in Mancos. (Courtesy, Center for Southwest Studies, Fort Lewis College)

"After traversing the frightfully rugged trails of the San Juan and La Plata Mountains, therefore, a portion of our party came out on the southern margin of the mountains, and, despite the smoldering hostility of the Indians, with which the region was filled, headed southward into the long deserted canons. There were five of us altogether—Mr. W. H. Jackson (from whose skillful camera came many of the illustrations that grace my present text), the famous Captain John Moss, who went with us as "guide, philosopher, and friend," myself, and two mule packers.

The trail led from Parrott City, then a nameless prospect camp, washing gold without a thought of the silver ledges to be developed there, over to Merritt's pleasant ranch on the upper Rio Mancos, then across rolling grass lands and through groves of magnificent pines, a distance of about fifteen miles. Spending one night at the ranch, sunrise the next morning found us eager to enter the portals of the canon and the precincts of the area within which glorious discoveries in anthropology allured our imagination and made light the toil and privation of the undertaking."

THE CREST OF THE CONTINENT
Ernest Ingersoll, 1885

Montezuma National Forest Supervisor's office in Mancos, June, 1915-note calendar on wall. (Courtesy, San Juan National Forest)

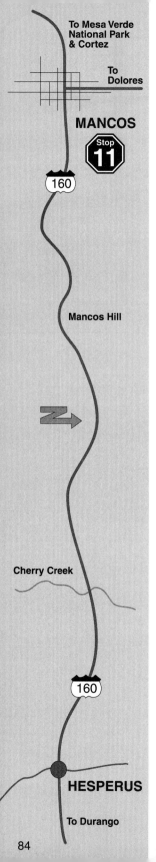

To Mesa Verde
National Park
& Cortez

To
Dolores

MANCOS

Stop
11

160

Mancos Hill

N →

Cherry Creek

160

● HESPERUS

To Durango

Mancos

"Merritt's pleasant ranch on the upper Rio Mancos" was one of the first in the Mancos Valley. The first modern settlers arrived that year, 1874, not to become ranchers but to prospect for gold in the nearby La Plata Mountains. By the end of the year, several prospectors had recognized that the rolling grasslands and magnificent groves of pines were a likelier source of profit than were the Silver Mountains. Each year more ranching and farming families came into the verdant valley.

The townsite of Mancos was laid out in 1881 and a post office was established there that year. Just south of Mancos the community of Webber was established in 1882 by members of the Church of Latter Day Saints (Mormon). The Mormon families came into the Mancos Valley from Bluff in southeastern Utah and spread out from Webber to settle more of the Mancos and La Plata valleys. The descendants of those first Mormon pioneers continue to live on the family farms established in the 1880s.

San Juan National
Forest ranger surveying
grazing plot, 1926.
(Courtesy, San Juan
National Forest)

A Quaker family, the Wetherills, arrived in the valley in 1881 and settled the Alamo Ranch on the Mancos River a few miles below Mancos. The Wetherill brothers grazed their cattle on top of Mesa Verde, then a part of Ute Reservation. Acting on instructions from the Utes, the Wetherill brothers "discovered" the spectacular cliff dwellings on Mesa Verde in 1888. The Wetherills became outfitters for the growing numbers of visitors wanting to see the ruins and went on to become famous in the annals of Southwestern archaeology.

Early Mancos.
(Courtesy, Colorado
Historical Society,
Neg. #F36,415)

STOP 11 - MANCOS

MANCOS VISITOR CENTER

The Mancos Visitor Center is located just south of Highway 160 at the intersection with Highway 184. It is open from May 1 to October 31 and features a historic display including photographs and items from early settler families and the early ranching, mining, railroad, and farming days in the Mancos River Valley. Self guided tour maps of historic buildings in Mancos may become available in 1994. The Visitor Center includes a display on the future of Mancos. Hours are 9 a.m. to 6 p.m. daily. Admission is free and voluntary contributions accepted. Elevation 7,008 feet above sea level.

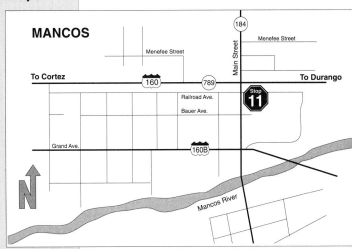

Development of the Mancos Valley was slow until the arrival there of the Rio Grande Southern in 1891. From Mancos, the route of the Rio Grande Southern turned northwest toward the town of Dolores. The coming of the railroad brought an air of permanence and stability to the ten-year-old town. Mancos was the nearest rail stop to Mesa Verde and soon took on the title of "Gateway to Mesa Verde" to the Mesa Verde bound visitors who arrived there by train each year.

MANCOS

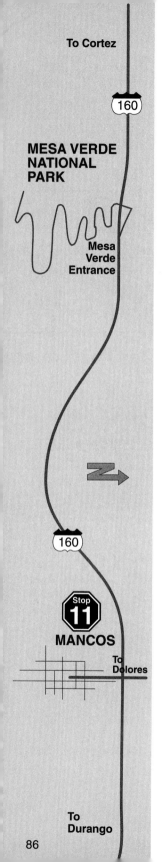

To Cortez

160

MESA VERDE NATIONAL PARK

Mesa Verde Entrance

N →

160

Stop 11

MANCOS

To Dolores

To Durango

Mancos to Mesa Verde

In 1951, sixty years after the Rio Grande Southern reached Mancos, the beleaguered rail company went out of business. Declining mining production in the mountains along with modern highways and truck transport, were too much competition for a railroad that had struggled since the repeal of the Sherman Silver Purchasing Act in 1893. By the end of 1951, railroad salvage crews had hauled away the last iron rails and today few visible traces remain of the Rio Grande Southern Railroad.

Today the Skyway through Mancos is on top of the railroad grade. One block south of the Skyway are the historic business structures along Grand Avenue. The mansion visible from the Skyway was built by George Bauer, a German immigrant and successful nineteenth century Mancos merchant.

From Mancos, the Skyway continues west toward Cortez. Seven and one-half miles (12 km) west of Mancos, on top of a low divide, the Skyway passes the entrance to Mesa Verde National Park. By the late 1890s looters from near and far were destroying the irreplaceable cliff dwellings of Mesa Verde, and many more ruins in the area, in search of artifacts to sell to collectors around the world. The Colorado Federation of Women's Clubs began a campaign, led by tireless women from the San Juan Country, to save the ruins. Congress created Mesa Verde National Park in 1906 out of part of the Ute Mountain Ute Reservation and the Utes were given Sleeping Ute Mountain to the west in exchange for land taken for the park. At the same time that the park was created, Congress passed the Antiquities Act of 1906, making it illegal to damage archaeological

A Ute wedding scene on the Wetherill brothers' Alamo Ranch, Mancos. (Courtesy, Colorado Historical Society. Neg. # 36408)

Cliff Palace, Mesa Verde National Park, before excavation and stabilization. (Courtesy, Colorado Historical Society. Neg. # 4253 photograph by William Henry Jackson)

sites on any public lands or to remove artifacts from them. The women of Colorado had achieved a significant victory for preservation of the state's past. Mesa Verde National Park is now designated by UNESCO as a World Cultural Heritage Site.

MESA VERDE NATIONAL PARK

Pueblo Indians farmed the mesa tops in what is now Mesa Verde National Park from A.D. 500 to A.D. 1300. Visitors to the Park may tour early pithouses and late cliffdwellings for a first hand look at the changes which took place in Puebloan architecture and culture over time. A museum on Chapin Mesa exhibits the ceramics and other objects from the daily life of a people who treasured beauty in everything around them.

Call (303) 529-4461 or 529-4463 for more information. Allow plenty of time to see all of the ancient villages of Mesa Verde. Lodging is available in the Park and in nearby Cortez and Mancos.

Montezuma Lumber Company loads ponderosa logs near Dolores, 1939. (Courtesy, San Juan National Forest)

MESA VERDE TO CORTEZ

Descending the low divide, one sees the vast expanse of the Great Sage Plain to the west and the Abajo Mountains in Utah. Here the Skyway enters the Montezuma Valley. Ten miles (16 km) west of Mancos the Skyway passes a year round Colorado Department of Transportation rest stop with a full view of Sleeping Ute Mountain at the western end of the Montezuma Valley. An interpretive sign at the rest stop recounts the ancient legend of Sleeping Ute Mountain.

Sixteen miles (25.6 km) west of Mancos, the Skyway enters Cortez at the junction of Highways 160 and 145. From here, the Skyway turns north toward the Anasazi Heritage Center & Dolores.

The ruin described in 1874 by the noted photographer William Henry Jackson is now preserved in Yucca House National Monument a few miles south of Cortez. It is only one of hundreds of ancient Puebloan farm communities found throughout the Montezuma Valley, the Great Sage Plain, and on Mesa Verde.

W.H. JACKSON

"Immediately adjoining the spring, on the right as we face it from below, is the ruin of a great structure of some kind, about 100 feet square in exterior dimensions; a portion only of the wall upon the northern face remaining in its original position. The debris of the ruin now forms a great mound of crumbling rock, from 12 to 20 feet in height, overgrown with artimisia, but showing clearly, however, its rectangular structure, adjusted

William Henry Jackson and his assistants photographed the Rocky Mountains from 1870 to 1878 for the U.S. Geological Survey, Hayden Expedition. (Courtesy, University of New Mexico Art Museum; Gift of Beaumont Newhall)

approximately to the four points of the compass. Inside this square is a circle, about 60 feet in diameter, deeply depressed in the center.... Upon the same level as this ruin, and extending back some distance, were grouped line after line of foundations and mounds.... Below the above group, some 200 yards distant, is another great wall, enclosing a space of about 200 feet square.... It was only a portion extending out into the plains.... The town built around this spring is nearly a square mile in extent, the larger and more enduring buildings in the center, while all about are scattered and grouped the remnants of smaller structures comprising the suburbs".

Ancient Ruins in Southwest Colorado
HAYDEN'S EIGHTH ANNUAL REPORT W.H. Jackson, 1874

Navajo student at Fort Lewis,
Hesperus. (Courtesy,
Colorado Historical Society.
Neg. # F36409)

Working cow camp in the San Juan
Mountains, 1930's. (Courtesy, San Juan
National Forest)

Winter on a homestead in the Montezuma Valley. (Courtesy, Colorado Historical Society. Neg. # F36411)

CORTEZ

CORTEZ

Cortez, in the center of the Montezuma Valley, is the second largest community on the San Juan Skyway. It is the only surviving community never served by a railroad and it is the only town not located along a river. Cortez boasts a historic engineering achievement of its own; if it wasn't on a river it would bring a river to it.

Modern settlement of the Montezuma Valley began in the 1870s and a small community grew up around the only permanent water source, Mitchell Springs, south of Cortez. The fertile soils of the valley attracted hopeful farm families, but the lack of water hindered profitable farming. The Dolores River Valley to the north is nearly 1,000 feet higher than the adjacent Montezuma Valley. The solution to drought would be to drill a tunnel between the two valleys and divert Dolores River water onto the parched farms on the lower slopes of the Montezuma Valley.

The original Montezuma Water Company was organized in 1885. The townsite of Cortez was laid out in 1886 by investors in the water company. The new town was high and dry. Water hauled from Mitchell Springs cost as much as 50 cents a barrel.

Ute rock art in the Ute Mountain Tribal Park. (Courtesy, San Juan National Forest)

The Montezuma Valley near Cortez with the La Plata Mountains and Mesa Verde in the background. (Courtesy, Colorado Historical Society. Neg. # 36410)

Work began on the tunnel in 1887 along with a network of canals to deliver water to the farms. Water from the Dolores River reached Cortez on July 4, 1890. The people of Mitchell Springs moved into Cortez. The irrigation system continued to expand. An additional canal was constructed from the Dolores River and flumes, one more than a mile long, were built to carry water across the many canyons that crease the valley slopes. By 1955 the system, now owned by the Montezuma Valley Irrigation Company, included the tunnel, two reservoirs, 25 canals and laterals more than 175 miles in length.

Dam to divert water from the Dolores River into the Montezuma Valley. (Courtesy, Colorado Historical Society. Neg. # F36414)

CORTEZ

McPhee Reservoir was completed in the 1980s and thousands more acres of farmland received irrigation water.

Today Cortez is known as the "Archaeological Center of the United States", for the many nearby ruins which are open to the public and where innovative archaeological research continues into the future. Within an hour's drive of Cortez are Mesa Verde National Park, Hovenweep National Monument, the Crow Canyon Archaeological Center, Escalante Ruin and the Anasazi Heritage Center, Lowry Ruin, and the Ute Mountain Ute Tribal

STOP 12 - CORTEZ

THE CORTEZ C.U. CENTER

**Operated in cooperation with the University of Colorado (CU), the Cortez C.U. Center is located at 25 North Market Street. It is open Monday through Saturday in summer and Monday through Friday in winter. Permanent exhibits feature area archaeology and traveling exhibits cover a variety of topics in the arts and sciences. Evening programs every night during the summer and at least once weekly during the winter. The adjacent outdoor Cultural Park features local Native American cultures and programs during the summer. Summer hours are 10 a.m. to approximately 9 p.m. Winter hours are 10 a.m. to 5 p.m. Admission to exhibits and most programs is free. Voluntary contributions accepted.
Elevation 6201 feet.**

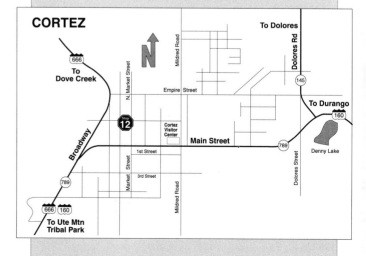

Park. The Tribal Park, 18 miles (28.8 km) south of Cortez, is unique because visitors are taken to excellently preserved cliff dwellings by knowledgeable Ute Mountain Ute Indian guides. Visitors learn about Ute cultures as well as ancient Puebloan cultures.

Cortez is the gateway to modern Native American cultures as well. Ute Mountain Ute Tribal headquarters are at Towaoc, twelve miles south of town. In addition to the Ute Mountain Ute Tribal Park, visitors are attracted to Towaoc by its new casino. Just south and west of the Ute Mountain Ute Reservation is the vast Navajo Nation in Arizona, New Mexico, and Utah.

Dolores Water Tunnel. (Courtesy, Bureau of Reclamation)

Early Cortez. (Courtesy, Colorado Historical Society. Neg. # F36416)

EPILOGUE

The story of the San Juan Skyway is both ancient and modern. Modern history began here little more than a century ago. Modern cultures wreaked havoc on older Native cultures and on the natural environment. Forests were stripped away, rivers oozed grey with mill tailings, smoke from smelters smudged the skies, and sheep and cattle grazed the grasslands to dust. Even the ancient and modern legacy of human history—hundreds of Puebloan ruins, historic mining structures, awesome railway trestles, whole Victorian mining camps, and farm homesteads—have been destroyed by greedy looters and vandals or have vanished in the path of "progress."

That has changed. The descendants of nineteenth century Native and European cultures, allied with determined newcomers, have banded together to preserve the material and traditional legacy of all cultures along the Skyway and to restore the natural environment here as the communities of the San Juan Country move into the twenty-first century.

Not all the scars have healed, nor will they soon. But cultures are learning to benefit from one another and the streams run cleaner, the forests grow taller, and dawn comes to bluer skies than was the case just decades ago. The San Juan Skyway leads not only into the past, but into the future as well.

Recommended Reading

Mallory Hope Ferrell, **THE RIO GRANDE SOUTHERN RAILROAD**, Pruett Publishing, Boulder.

David Lavendar, **A ROCKY MOUNTAIN FANTASY, TELLURIDE, COLORADO**, San Miguel County Historical Society, Telluride.

Allen Nossaman, **MANY MORE MOUNTAINS**, Volumes 1 and 2, Sundance Publications, Denver.

David P. Smith, **OURAY, CHIEF OF THE UTES**, Wayfinder Press, Ouray.

Duane Smith, **ROCKY MOUNTAIN BOOM TOWN, A HISTORY OF DURANGO**, University of New Mexico Press, Albuquerque.

Ian M. Thompson, **TREASURES OF THE PAST: THE ANCIENT VILLAGES OF MESA VERDE**, (A Video Cassette), Mesa Verde Museum Association, Mesa Verde National Park.

Ian M. Thompson, **FOUR CORNERS COUNTRY**, University of Arizona Press, Tucson.

Ian M. Thompson, **THE ESCALANTE COMMUNITY**, Southwest Natural and Cultural Heritage Association, Albuquerque.

About the Author

Cortez writer Ian (Sandy) Thompson has been editor of THE SILVERTON STANDARD, associate editor of THE DURANGO HERALD, and executive director of the Crow Canyon Archaeological Center. He is author of FOUR CORNERS COUNTRY, University of Arizona Press, and writes a column for the SUNDAY DURANGO HERALD. His family has lived along the San Juan Skyway for four generations.

Photography Credits

Photography for this book has been supplied by a number of sources including: the Colorado State Historical Society, the Center for Southwest Studies at Fort Lewis College, the La Plata County Historical Society, the San Juan National Forest, the San Juan County Historical Society, the Bureau of Reclamation, the Anasazi Heritage Center, the Strater Hotel, the Telluride Historical Society, the Galloping Goose Historical Society, the University of New Mexico Art Museum, H. Jackson Clark, the Denver Public Library and Trimble Hot Springs.

Headed for the low country as winter approaches. (Courtesy, La Plata County Historical Society)

House at the Yankee Girl Mine at the ghost town of Guston on Red Mountain Pass, 1886. (Courtesy, Colorado Historical Society. Neg. #F25,976)

ACKNOWLEDGEMENTS

Acknowledgements

The Fort Lewis College Office of Community Services is dedicated to working with communities, agencies, businesses, individuals and other partners in helping preserve the heritage of the San Juan Country in southwestern Colorado. This guide is an example of such a partnership.

Recent photo of Artwork's staff.
(Courtesy, La Plata County Historical Society)

The idea for this guide came from Colorado Preservation, Inc., who first worked with the Southwest Colorado Travel Region in developing the concept. Funding assistance was provided by the Colorado Scenic and Historic Byway Commission/Federal Highway Administration, US West, San Juan National Forest Heritage Resources Program, and the Colorado Historical Society. Dianna Litvak of the Colorado Historical Society provided valuable guidance on the characteristics of effective travel guides.

Constructive reviews of the text were provided by Ken Francis, Mark Franklin, Ann Bond, Allen Nossaman, Dick Ostergaard, Jill Seyfarth and Duane Smith. Rebecca Lintz of the Colorado Historical Society, Catherine Conrad of the Center for Southwest Studies at Fort Lewis College, Allen Nossaman of the San Juan Historical Society and Robert McDaniel of the La Plata County Historical Society were among those who helped with the photography research. Paul Dunn and his staff at Artworks in Durango made the design and production of this book a work of love. And the assistance of the volunteers and staffs of museums along the San Juan Skyway was invaluable.

Color Covers: Courtesy, San Juan National Forest,
Photos by Richard F. Ostergaard.
Sepiatones: Old car- Courtesy, San Juan National Forest &
Dolores town- Courtesy, Galloping Goose Historical Society,
Photo by William Henry Jackson

(Courtesy, Center for Southwest Studies, Fort Lewis College)